EMBROIDERY MAGIC
on
PATTERNED FABRICS

EMBROIDERY MAGIC
on
PATTERNED FABRICS

by Betty Parker & Edith Martin

CHARLES SCRIBNER'S SONS NEW YORK

PHOTOGRAPHIC CREDITS

Ed Carroll, American Photo Service: black and white photos on pages 23, 25, 26, 27, 28, 30, 33, 36, 42, 43, 49, 53, 55, 56, 58, 61, 62, 66, 69, 70, 71, 72, 75, 76, 77, 80, 81, 82, 83, 87, 89, 90, 91, 92, 105, 107; color plates 6, 7, 8, 11, 12, 13, 14, 15, 18, 19, 20, 21, 25, 26, 27, 29, 30.

David O. Johnson, Princeton Polychrome Press: black and white photos on pages ii, 16, 19, 20, 21, 31, 35, 37, 50, 51, 63, 65, 79; color plates 2, 3, 4, 5, 10, 16, 17, 22, 23, 24, 28.

Library of Congress Cataloging in Publication Data

Parker, Betty.
    Embroidery magic on patterned fabrics.
    Includes index.
    1. Embroidery. 2. Textile fabrics. I. Martin,
Edith, joint author. II. Title.
TT770.P24   746.4′4   76-14976
ISBN 0-684-14722-X

1 3 5 7 9 11 13 15 17 19 MD / C 20 18 16 14 12 10 8 6 4 2

Printed in the United States of America

CONTENTS

Foreword   xi

Instant Heirlooms   3

Color—Your Personal Expression   11

Pillows Unlimited   15

    Geometric Jacquard Pillow   16

    Traditional Floral Cotton Pillow   18

    A Design-Perfect Pillow   19

    Pink and Orange Pillows   20

Matelassé   22

An Easy Working Surface   24

Personal Bagatelles   25

Needlecase   25

Eyeglass Cases   26

Stitchery Sampler   27

A Geometric Sample   28

Traditional Velvet   30

One Material, Two Uses   31

    A Stool   31

    A Wastepaper Basket   32

The Versatility of Brocade   34

    A Stool   34

    A Pincushion   36

    Flowered Satin Brocade Pillow   37

Beautiful Bedrooms   38
    Handsome Headboard   38
    Bedspreads from Fascinating Fabrics   39
Variations on a Theme   42
    A Box   42
    A Desk Blotter   43
Tremendous Trifles   44
    Matchboxes   44
    Telephone-Book Cover   45
    Folding Jewel Case   46
Enhancing Unusual Motifs   48
    Zuni Apron   48
    White Sheath with Border   50
    Hand-Woven Dress   51
A Super Sweater   52
The Wonderful World of Gingham   54
    Scallop Shell   56
    An Apron with Wings   58
    An Apron with Daisies   60
    Apron with a Checked Border   62
    Wastepaper Basket   63
Imaginative Inserts for Ready-Mades   64
    Ice Bucket with Key Design   64
    A Wall Sconce   67
    A Tray   67
    Diamonds and Daisies   69
Perfect Presents   70
    Table Talk   70
    Blanket for a Baby   71
    A Glamorous Towel   72
    Girl's Sunsuit   73

Boy's Sunsuit   74
A Scarf   74
Playing-Card Case   76
Moiré Book Cover   77
Enhancing Ready-Mades   78
A Decorated Jewel Box   78
Straw Hat   79
An Adaptable Belt   80
Bedroom Slippers   81
A Bright Blouse   82
A Checked Dress   83
Evening Skirt with Flair   84
A Yellow Tablecloth   85
A Blue Tablecloth   86
Sheets and Pillow cases   86
Sheer Curtains   88
Net Curtains   90
Linen   91
Chintz   93
Contemporary Chintz Print   93
Charcoal Linen   96
A Pair of Spanish Chairs   97
The Elegance of Ecclesiastical Embroidery   101
Golden Crosses   101
The Lamb of God   102
Miscellaneous Medley   104
Sturdy Luggage Rack   104
A Tote Bag   104
Portable Magazine Rack   107
Glossary of Stitches   109
Index   115

ILLUSTRATIONS IN COLOR

Following page 4:

    Plate 1   Brocade with wool embroidery
    Plate 2   Flowers on apricot satin brocade
    Plate 3   Silk embroidered seat on gold and black chair
    Plate 4   Pink and orange modern design
    Plate 5   Floral cotton print
    Plate 6   Gray and gold pattern with embroidered accents
    Plate 7   Celadon chintz with massed flowers
    Plate 8   Strong pink embroidery on charcoal linen
    Plate 9   Strawberries and flowers on yellow chintz
    Plate 10   Coordinated headboard and bedspread
    Plate 11   Detail of the headboard
    Plate 12   Matchboxes
    Plate 13   A jewel box
    Plate 14   Telephone-book cover
    Plate 15   Tracing for brocade seat shown in Plate 1

Following page 100:

    Plate 16   Contemporary brocade on antique Spanish chair
    Plate 17   Second seat for Spanish chairs
    Plate 18   Folding jewel case
    Plate 19   Children's sunsuits
    Plate 20   Blue tablecloth
    Plate 21   Yellow tablecloth
    Plate 22   Tray cover
    Plate 23   Luggage rack
    Plate 24   Portable magazine rack
    Plate 25   Floral chintz, plain
    Plate 26   Floral chintz with added embroidery
    Plate 27   Evening skirt
    Plate 28   Taos dress
    Plate 29   The Lamb of God
    Plate 30   Golden crosses

FOREWORD

WOVEN FABRICS have been variously decorated with stitchery since the Stone Age. Many embroideries and many books, each embodying the style and philosophy of its age, survive from past centuries. Probably as many men and women are embroidering today as ever before, and as many books on the subject are being published, but this book has a new slant in that it expands the idea of embroidering on patterned fabrics.

This imaginative book by two contemporary embroideresses is delightfully oriented toward this decade's concern with the quality of life. As the authors explain, in breezy, non-dictorial style, embroidery can be play of the most delightful sort, exercising the embroiderer's imagination and expressing his personal taste and resulting in unique objects personal to him and his life-style.

I find *Embroidery Magic on Patterned Fabrics* a most cheering expression of a positive aspect of the spirit of the '70s and salute the authors for their contribution to human happiness.

JEAN MAILEY
Associate Curator
The Metropolitan Museum of Art
Textile Study Room

EMBROIDERY MAGIC
on
PATTERNED FABRICS

Instant Heirlooms

A new technique to unlock your embroidery imagination

EVER SINCE the first cave woman started an interior decorating trend by draping a bearskin over a boulder, women have derived pleasure from creating articles of usefulness and beauty for their homes.

Today the urge to "make something" is in full cry and even the local supermarket carries kits ranging from pincushions to room-sized rugs. It is easy to forget that our forebears had to raise the lamb, shear it, cord the wool, spin the yarn, and gather the berries to dye the thread before they could even anticipate the pleasure of actually hooking the needed rug. The same held true for bed-spreads and clothing—first the linen threads to be spun, then the cloth to be woven, yarns dyed, etc., while planting the corn, tend-ing the pigs, working in the home, and caring for the children. Even the glamorous ladies of upper rank, sewing away in some drafty castle, made tapestries more to keep out the cold than for their aesthetic value.

Today's contemporary woman has an Aladdin's wealth of fabrics to choose from before beginning her own personalized masterpiece.

3

She may want to make something for the children or a gift for "someone who has everything." Or, as is primarily the case, she may want to create an article of lasting beauty for her home—an article that (she hopes) will be treasured and honored (reverently) from generation to generation.

In Victorian times a household with an abundance of daughters was equipped with bedspreads, wall hangings, chair seats, tablecloths, and rugs. The younger girls were kept out of mischief by compulsory sewing of samplers to decorate the walls. Even today in Latin American countries young ladies of marriageable age do miles of needlepoint for ornately covered chairs. Doing eight dining-room chairs in petit point is as good as having a duenna. The poor girl simply can't steal away for forbidden fruit, as it quickly becomes apparent that no further stitches have been taken and she is therefore suspect!

For those of us who want purely to *create*, the opportunities are endless. Martha Washington, while waiting for George to come home (and she had quite a wait), worked a series of chair seats in bargello for their home at Mount Vernon. She probably admonished George to remove his sword before dinner lest he snag some of her stitches.

In the early 1900s silk was imported from Spitalsfield, England, to adorn the wealthier ladies (and gentlemen) of the Colonies. There are many outfits on view at the Fabric Museum of Deerfield Village in Deerfield, Massachusetts, which show the delicacy and richness of the dress of our forebears. Today, we can do without boned waists and frothing lace jabots that would fall into the cake mix, but we welcome the idea of using fabrics with a raised pattern to embellish the clothing and furniture of our contemporary lives.

An evening skirt of silk damask with embroidered roses would cause as much delighted comment today as the French and Spitalsfield silks did in the eighteenth or nineteenth century. To make

Plate 1   Blue brocade chair seat worked in white, plum, and two shades of green. Tracing design is shown on Plate 15. See pages 5 and 6.

Plate 2   Embroidered flowers on
apricot satin brocade. See page 37.

Plate 3   The same design as
Plate 1, worked in silk. See pages
5 and 8.

Plate 4   Pink and orange pillow in a modern design. See pages
20 and 21.

Plate 5   Embroidery picks up
the design on a floral cotton print.
See page 18.

Plate 6   Gray and gold fabric with embroidered accents. See pages 41 and 84.

Plate 7   Celadon chintz with pink flowers. See pages 40 and 84.

Plate 8   Strong pink embroidery on charcoal linen. See pages 39, 84, and 96.

Plate 9   Strawberries and flowers on yellow chintz.
See pages 40 and 84.

Plate 10   Bedspread and matching headboard. See page 38.

Plate 11   Detail of the headboard.

Plate 12 A variety of matchboxes. See page 44.

Plate 13 An elegant jewel box highlighted with silver thread. See page 78.

Plate 14 An embroidered cover greatly improves the appearance of a telephone book. See page 45.

Plate 15   The tracing for the design shown on Plate 1. See page 6.

such an outfit would not involve an enormous outlay—to find it ready-made would be almost impossible and utterly exorbitant. After perusing this book we hope you'll be encouraged to sit down and *create*. The key to these projects is to use only a little money but a lot of imagination.

The idea of embroidering an already patterned fabric is not new, but we hope our concept is new. Our idea is simply to create an heirloom with the maximum effect using a minimum of effort. There is no drawing, no time-consuming transferring of designs to be done, as the pattern is already on the fabric, ready and waiting. The idea may be applied to large or small projects. An eyeglass case measuring 3 x 5 inches or a headboard 20 x 60—all it takes is a bit of imagination. (See color inserts.) We show examples of useful articles such as wastepaper baskets as well as some purely decorative silken pillows. The idea in a nutshell is this: take a fabric with a clearly discernible pattern and raise part of the pattern to the prominence of a third dimension by embroidering it. No drawing skills are needed, as the design is already woven into the fabric. The chef-d'oeuvre of this book is the chair seat shown in color plate 1. It shows a piece of pale-blue brocade with the design embroidered in white, plum, and two shades of green. It was worked in wool yarns after a tracing was made and the colors were decided upon (see color plate 15 for the tracing in color). This piece was subsequently mounted onto the slip seat of an antique black chair. The white flowers tie in beautifully with the mother-of-pearl inserts in the frame.

As two chairs exist another seat was made by working the same motif but using silk yarns for interest and change of feeling. As you will see from the photograph in plate 3, it is the variety of stitches and the switching from woolen to silken yarns that give a totally different "look" to the finished seat. All the stitches are embroidery stitches and are shown enlarged in the back of the book. Some stitches are incredibly easy and some are for the more advanced needleworker. No one stitch is mandatory—you may prefer to choose your own after having viewed our samples. This is to be *fun*, not *a chore*. These are only suggestions, not rules. This book is for pleasure and to help unlock your imagination. Your own personal trick may be to use different-weight silks, cottons, or wools to achieve a particular effect. You may use the same simple stitch over and over and gain variety only by changing the colors. Or, even simpler, you may use the same stitch, working some in wool and some in silk, thereby gaining a totally different effect.

The brocade on the two chair seats was woven in definite floral groupings. We first studied it carefully to decide which parts to highlight. A simple way to decide this is to lay a sheet of tracing paper over the brocade and with a felt-tip pen outline the overall design. You can then color in the leaves and flowers with watercolor or crayons. It's a lot easier to change your mind on tracing paper than it is to pull out stitches once they've been sewn. (The tracing shown in color plate 15 will clearly demonstrate this point.) Quite often the painted tracing will lead to further experimentation with colors and effects and the results will astound you. The joy is that the drawing has already been done and all you have to do is to give an added depth to the flowers and/or leaves that appeal to you the most. It's easy and yet incredibly effective and goes very quickly. Unlike needlepoint, you have no acres of background to labor over after you've finished the fun part of the design—it's all done before you start!

The chair seat in plate 1 was done with wool yarn—mostly single strand. The flowers were outlined in *satin stitch* with the plum-colored accents in *split stitch*. Some of the centers and buds were worked in a *double cross stitch*. The leaves are formed by a single strand of wool *chain stitch* done in two tones of green—the same for the stems. The ribbons are composed of white and plum *chain stitch*. The bowknot is *satin stitch*, tied down with large *cross stitch*, and the *cross stitch* is tied down, in turn, with another small *cross stitch* (one on top of the other).

As the diagram is symmetrical, the colors have been keyed on one side only.

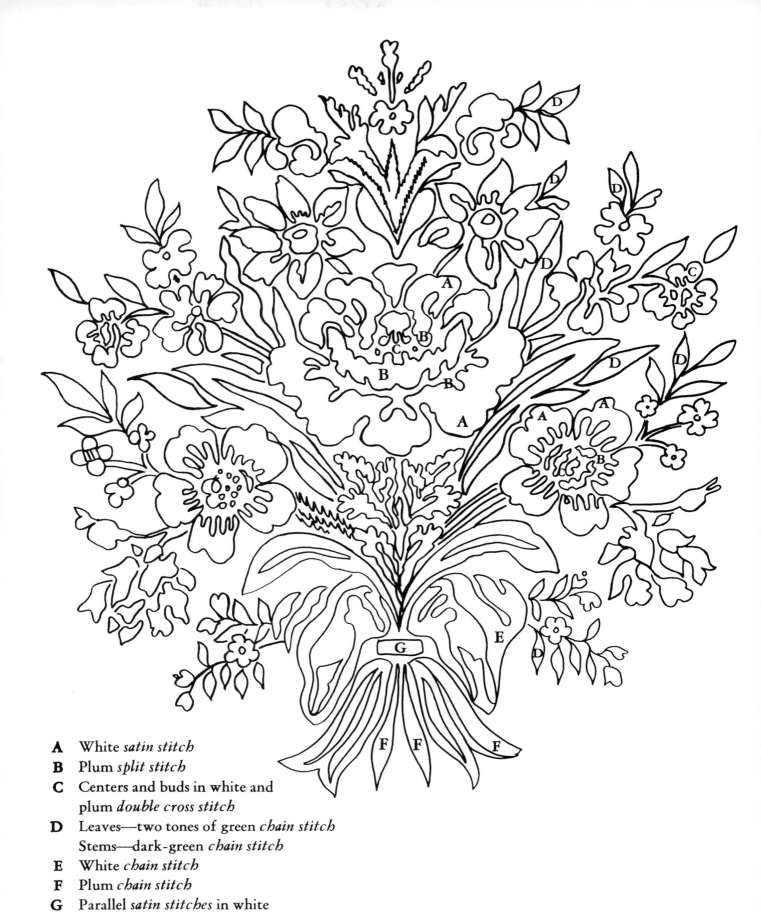

A White *satin stitch*

B Plum *split stitch*

C Centers and buds in white and
  plum *double cross stitch*

D Leaves—two tones of green *chain stitch*
  Stems—dark-green *chain stitch*

E White *chain stitch*

F Plum *chain stitch*

G Parallel *satin stitches* in white
  tied down by large *cross stitch*
  with another small stitch on top

As you will note from the photographs, silken and mercerized cottons give a lighter and airier feeling than the same stitches worked with woolen yarn. Therefore, decide before you start whether the piece of furniture demands a country (wool) look or city (silken) air. Also, the thickness of your yarn will make a visual difference. In all cases we will tell you whether we used one strand or more in spots where a lighter or heavier effect was needed.

Whenever you have large areas of embroidery, or the article is one that will undergo hard usage, make sure you use stitches that will not readily "lift" or "snag." For example, it would have been easier to use a plain *cross stitch*, but a chair seat gets a lot of wear and tear; therefore we decided that a *tied-down cross stitch* was called for to avoid future anguish and repair work.

By using silk thread and different stitches we varied the appearance of the seat on the companion chair. (See color plate 3.)

The flowers were outlined in two strands of white silk by using a *buttonhole stitch*. The shading consists of three strands of plum-colored silk in *chain stitch*. The centers of some of the flowers are *buttonhole*: small dots in the center of some are *cross stitch*, some are *satin*, and some are *detached chain*. (By looking at the stitch diagrams in the back you'll be able to recognize the difference.)

All the stems were done in *twisted chain* using three strands of silk in two tones of green. The leaves are two-tone green, using three strands of silk in *Cretan stitch*. The center grouping of light-colored leaves directly under the central blossom was outlined with *stem stitch* and has random *chain stitches* for added interest.

The white ribbons were worked in *twisted chain*, the plum accents in *Cretan*; the bowknot is formed by *padded satin* with a *herringbone stitch tied down*.

We think the results justify placing these chairs in our heirloom category.

A   *Buttonhole stitch* in white
B   Shading of flowers in plum *chain stitch*
C   *Buttonhole stitch* in green
D   *Satin stitch* in green
E   *Twisted chain* stitch for dark-green stems

As the diagram is symmetrical, the colors have been keyed on one side only.

F *Cretan stitch* for dark-green leaves

G *Cretan stitch* for light-green leaves

H Bowknot in white *twisted chain* stitch

I Padded *satin* with tied down *herringbone stitch*

J *Cretan stitch* in plum

This book is meant to stimulate the artist hidden in every one of us. It shows clearly how to make an heirloom almost instantly. The major work has been done by the fabric manufacturer; you add the frills—rather like putting the icing on the cake. However, as you would start with a good cake, so you should start with a good piece of fabric. Cheap, sleazy stuff is not worth a tuppenny-bit. Mill-end outlets will sell a yard of good brocade for as little as three or four dollars; with an overlay of silken or woolen stitches, the resultant chair seat or pillow is positively jeweled and a thing of beauty. And, a "thing of beauty is a joy forever" (or so we believe).

Color—
Your Personal Expression

COLOR IS THE ESSENCE of all that's beautiful in nature and it is hard to improve upon nature's color combinations. The pure white of a gull silhouetted against a clear blue sky, or floating on an indigo sea, presents an unforgettable picture. The autumn forest ablaze with the glowing glory of hundreds of shades of red and gold, and punctuated by the quiet green of hemlocks, makes one pause in happy and peaceful contemplation. Nature gives us a magnificent palette of colors to choose from and we learn from just looking around us.

The peasant costumes of olden days were a mass of brightly colored embroideries and brought a cheery touch to the festivals and Sunday church outings that enlivened the people's extremely hard lives. The dark, gloomy castle strongholds guarding the hilltops were relieved by the addition of large tapestries—not only to keep out the cold but to bring in the beauty and light and color of the outdoors. This book is not only aimed at creating necessities of life; it is hoped that these worked examples will release a stream of your own ideas that will excite, encourage, and enrich your leisure

11

hours. The proper use of color may come easily to some, but others will not find it so simple. That last word is a key one—that is, try to keep your combinations clear-cut and simple and, above all else, avoid a busy look. We can give you some cardinal rules to smooth your path, but experimentation on paper with watercolor or crayons will save a lot of time and woe.

Suppose we started off by saying, "Do not use yellow thread on yellow cotton." At first glance you might say, "But of course I wouldn't be so silly." However, you'd be wrong! Herein enters the question of relative textures—the relationships of silk or wool against cotton. A yellow *cotton* skirt printed with yellow daisies could be turned into a party outfit if the daisies were embroidered in either a matching or a stronger-toned yellow *silk* thread. With the attached leaves done in a solid *satin stitch*—thereby presenting a solid silken design—you'd end up with a truly beautiful article of clothing. Or, to hark back to the more peasanty air, all the daisies might be done in a kaleidoscope of colors making the skirt seem younger and more frivolous. Whatever you do, try to stay away from muddy colors—sad browns, gloomy grays, and blah blues. Even the Puritans got tired of their everlasting gray and lightened their suits and dresses with spanking white collars and cuffs.

We do not mean to imply that soft colors aren't to be used. There are times when a rose tone would be infinitely preferable to a fire-engine red. If possible, take your fabric with you when you shop for your yarns and threads and lay out the hanks on the material before you choose. Bear in mind that a single row of blue *chain stitch* is not going to appear as dark as the entire hank does while it is in your hand or lying on the cloth. Also, when using a gradation of shades, don't choose "dark, darker, darkest" but rather "not too dark, much darker, and darkest." In other words, make the difference between the shades be a true one, not a slight one, or it won't show up well and have the necessary impact on the fabric.

As you know, there is an entire classification of embroidery called "white work." It is literally white floss on white cotton or white yarn on white linen, etc., ad infinitum. Blue on blue, red on red, it doesn't matter—chances are the fabric will tell you what's right, and besides you know even better which color combination is going to please you and fit in with your decorating scheme. Recall how well the onion pattern on china has lasted over the years; it is a simple teaming of blue and white. Try not to have fussy or complicated color schemes except on rare occasions. If you have some red damask that you think is perfect for your dining-room chairs, think before you stitch. Realizing that your walls are light yellow and that the rug is a dark blue, you have two alternatives. You could embroider your pattern in a slightly darker red, which would give you a quiet but rich three-dimensional effect and would be extremely handsome, or you could use the same family of blue as the rug for a more startling result. But under no circumstances would you introduce green or yellow into the design or your room would end up looking like a neon jukebox!

There is more leeway in the use of varied colors when you are making articles for personal use than you have when adhering to a special decorating theme. Some of today's magazines for the homemaker show rooms that would make us quite dizzy. Every chair is upholstered in a different fabric, the walls glisten with metallic papers, and the ceilings are apt to be covered with calico. Instead, visit your local museum and sense the serenity of the old rooms reproduced there. The colors are muted (not faded; there is a definite difference), and each piece seems to complement its neighbor. The so-called Williamsburg colors used on walls are a case in point. They are soft and the furniture and fabrics show up well against their deliberately quiet tonal quality. In such a room the crewel work on chairs and bed hangings seems to glow and the entire room is full of charm, warmth, and peace. The only room where you can have a merry-go-round of color is a child's room. Children seem happiest surrounded by red trucks, black bears, yellow birds, and bright blue balls. Our friendly black-and-white panda (plate 24) is quite at home in such a gay setting, yet he'd be slightly out of place seated on our blue damask chair (color plate 3)! So don't labor over a Chinese silk pillow with ethereal cherry blossoms if you're making a pillow for your husband's den. Pick a masculine fabric that will go with his sofa or rug or wallpaper and try to emphasize on it one of the basic overall colors of his wallpaper or sofa covering. Then, even though the patterns of the fabric may be quite different from the slipcover, the two will complement each other and be at home together in the same room without clashing.

Pillows Unlimited

PILLOWS ARE VERSATILE. They can be soft, squishy bedmates or hard, round rocks of accent color on a formal sofa. They can be thrown by children, sat upon for TV, and they always sell well at church fairs. A pillow is a splendid starting point for a new embroidery project. You can do as much or as little as you wish and the results will be satisfying. You can take a year and a half doing an intricate pair of brocade pillows working in 49 different stitches and 149 shades of silk single-strand thread. Or you can whip up a new cretonne pillow between lunch and dinner using double strands of wool yarn and simple stitches. Even a ready-made pillow from a discount store can be dressed up in very little time. When the pillow is already made up this is slightly more difficult to do, as it is hard to start and end your threads invisibly. But it *can* be done, and effectively. To start your thread you have several alternatives. You can run it up under the fabric about the length of your needle and anchor it with two very small *back stitches* where the needle comes out. Then start your *chain* or *split* or *herringbone* directly on top of the first stitch and chances are it will never show. If you want to finesse the first anchoring stitch you can work over the thread (which is under the fabric) and thereby catch it and hold it in place. To end it you reverse the process.

15

GEOMETRIC JACQUARD PILLOW

This satin Jacquard pillow was not a ready-made find. Prowling through a remnant shop we were struck by the simplicity of this geometric design, with its clearly discernible rectangles, and thought it perfect for our purpose. We used a single strand of wool yarn in related shades of rose red to complement its pale-pink color.

To start with, the size of the pillow was decided upon and the center was marked with a pin and the design proceeded outward. The center rectangle has a *spiderweb* in rust and beige using a single strand of wool. The next central rectangles were done in plum-colored *squared filling* with *single stitches* to tie them down. The central motif is surrounded with a looping of *feather stitches*.

The next circle of rectangles is composed of *double diagonal squared filling*, using three different colors: plum, light rose, and deep rose.

The four outer rectangles were done in *squared filling*, and *French knots*, in plum and deep rose respectively, to give a finishing touch. The fabric is luxurious and soft enough for a bedroom, but the design and choice of strong colors make the overall result versatile enough for this pillow also to be used in the living room.

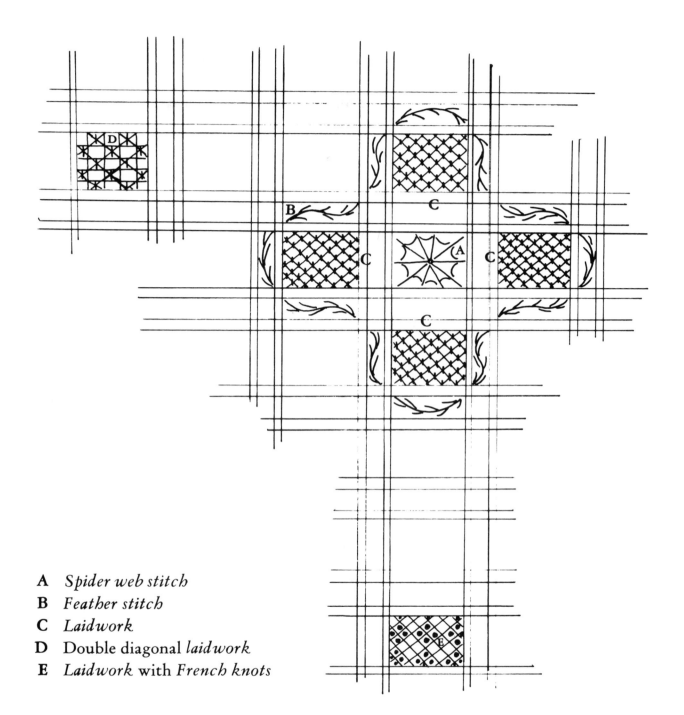

A *Spider web stitch*
B *Feather stitch*
C *Laidwork*
D Double diagonal *laidwork*
E *Laidwork* with *French knots*

TRADITIONAL FLORAL COTTON PILLOW

This beauty would be at home in any decor. The cotton has a formal flowery design printed in beige on a white ground. Looking from top to bottom you'll see that the central panel has flowers worked in groupings of three shades of deep pink and three shades of deep red. A single strand of wool was used in the *satin stitch*. The centers of the red flowers were done in *chain stitch* and the pink blossoms have clusters of yellow *French knots* and brown *cross stitches*. All the stems were worked in *Rumanian stitches* in a dark green, which shows up beautifully against the white background and gives necessary weight to balance the dark tones of the red and deep-pink flowers. (See plate 5.)

The leaves that appear solidly embroidered were done in four shades of green in *chain stitch*. The ribbon was outlined in two shades of dark brown in *twisted chain* and was subsequently filled in with dark-brown *French knots*.

The feathery accents outside the ribbon border were worked in a light brown using a *detached chain stitch*. The finished product is a splendid combination of lightness and strength because of an excellent mating of color and stitchery technique.

The parallel rows at each side consist of leaves outlined in two shades of green *stem stitch*. The veins of the leaves were embroidered in *chain stitch* in a rich dark brown. The larger flowers were again alternately worked in three shades of deep pink and dark red in the ever-effective *satin stitch*. The centers of these blooms, and the buds, have been filled in with *French knots*.

This particular fabric could be embroidered more simply for a more modern look. A single shade of dark-blue yarn (using the same stitches) would stand out on the white ground in a chinoiserie effect and give a totally different feeling to the pillows. This is the fun of doing your own creating. Given a well-designed fabric to work on, *you* are the artist and the result can cover a multitude of decorative concepts.

A DESIGN-PERFECT PILLOW

Velvets are gold mines for gift making. They come in silks and cottons, in plain and cut, with floral or geometric patterns, and they present endless possibilities.

This pillow is in quiet shades of grays, taupes, and white. Only a small amount of emphasis was needed and the glorification of the pattern was supplied by simply outlining the design in brown silk. Two strands were used in a *stem stitch*. After mounting, matching brown silk fringe was sewn around the edges. Couturier pillows for pennies!

PINK AND ORANGE PILLOWS

Home-decorating magazines are mouth-watering time killers. Gone are the days of stereotyped Louis XV rooms which were beautiful museum settings totally unfitted for a den mother and her active cookie-crumbling troop. Today's furniture may be a blend of antique and modern and the fabrics range from formal French silks to Aunt Jennie's quilt glued to the ceiling.

Usefulness seems to be the key word and not all rooms are silk-and-satin boudoirs where one fears to spill a drop of tea. Today's living areas have large, comfortable sofas and pillows, and hassocks are abundantly scattered around. If silk brocade is not your "thing," and you prefer a stronger, more contemporary appearance in your decorating, these cotton pillows are the answer to your prayers. No one could call their design old-fashioned, dull, or namby-pamby. It is definitely a modern design printed in clear pink and orange. It has a basically simple design of vertical and horizontal planes and we have embroidered two versions to show its versatility. The second example may be seen in color plate 4.

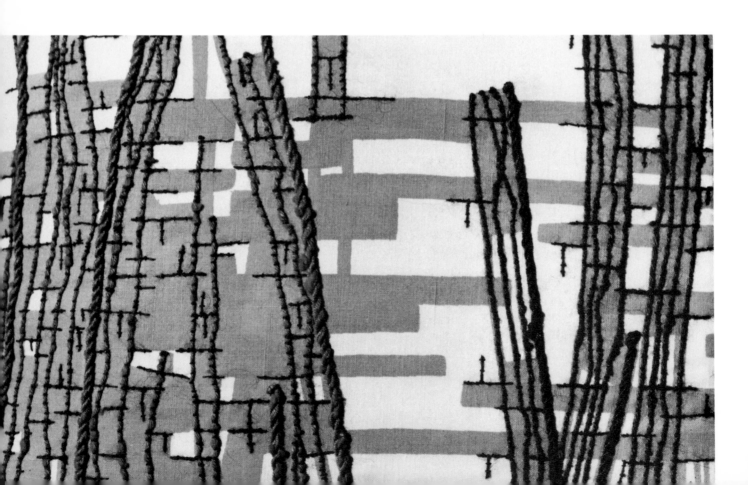

To duplicate that second pillow (starting from left to right), work the long lines in *stem stitch* using a single strand of fuchsia-colored wool yarn. The inside area is then worked in an interesting form of *herringbone stitch*. The honeycomb effect was attained by using two strands of yarn in the needle—one fuchsia and one pale green. The next side is the same only done in rust instead of fuchsia. This time the *herringbone* "honeycomb" was achieved by combining one strand of a deeper shade of rust with the green. Whether you prefer the terminology "modern" or "contemporary," these pillows have a very up-to-date air about them.

This pillow is the mate to the one shown above and opposite in black and white. To avoid boredom and to have a more interesting pair for the sofa, they were embroidered differently. They are obviously meant to be used in tandem but are, at the same time, strong enough to stand on their own.

On this one the heavy lines on the left were done in *couched* cording running diagonally. The other diagonal lines were *couched* with heavy rug yarn. The light horizontal lines were *couched* in a single strand of rust-colored crewel yarn. The right-hand side was done with the same stitches but using fuchsia yarns. The first pillow gained its interest from having eight different stitches. This one demonstrates the advisability of using different weights of yarn to achieve a needed variation. "Experimentation is the spice of life" in this particular embroidery game.

MATELASSÉ

To illustrate our embellishment idea we worked two flowers and three leaves on a monotone matelassé. This type of material would serve beautifully for chair seats, stools, or pillows. The pattern is already slightly raised and the additional height gained by the embroidery gives it a three-dimensional quality.

On the pale seafoam-green linen matelassé the veins of the leaves were worked in small *straight stitches* using a single strand of lemon-yellow wool. The leaves were outlined in light-green *satin stitch* and a few *satin stitches* in a medium blue were added for accent. The main stem of the tulip was done in a *chain stitch* in the same medium blue; the tulip was outlined in pale-pink *satin stitch* and the veins were composed of lemon-yellow *running stitches*.

The central flower was completely worked in *satin stitch*. The outer petals are teal blue, the inner petals medium blue with yellow silk centers worked with three strands of silk thread. The exact center was done in pale yellow single-strand wool yarn.

As you can see this delightful design is extraordinarily effective with only three simple stitches and a minimum of color variations. It would make an eye-catching pillow if worked in white silk with a few parts, such as the veins, centers and stems, embroidered in dark-green silk. This is the type of material that shows the most immediate results without much effort.

AN EASY WORKING SURFACE

Almost *anything* can be accomplished more easily and more quickly if you have the proper tools. This holds true whether you are building the Brooklyn Bridge or embroidering a needlecase. For our particular projects you need intangibles such as imagination and a willingness to try something new. The tangible needs are usually already at hand: good light, eyeglasses (if necessary), a hoop, and clean needles. One possession that we find indispensable is a work table large enough to accommodate yard goods, tracing papers, paints, yarns, and all the paraphernalia that one needs for creating masterpieces. Rather than mar your best bridge table we suggest getting a piece of ⅜-inch plywood cut into a 30 x 30- or 36 x 36-inch square. Either size will rest nicely on top of the average card table, but the slightly larger size is better if you're addicted to voluminous skirts or gargantuan pillows. Wipe the board well to make sure it hasn't a residue of plywood splinters from the cutting and then cover it with plain white contact paper. Make sure that it goes over all the edges (and sticks underneath) by at least 3 inches. This ensures a snagproof surface. Smooth the paper on evenly and watch out for bubbles, or overlooked splinters, as either one can cause your pen to "skitter" if you hit it when marking a pattern. When not needed, this working board can live under the bed or in a closet and is readily transportable from bedroom to ballroom or to whatever spot you prefer to call your workshop.

This board or a comparable surface is a must when working with light slippery fabrics. If you're young enough, you may like using the floor, but we have dogs and we found paw prints and a cocker spaniel soulfully seated in the middle of our fabric a distinct hazard.

Personal Bagatelles

NEEDLECASE

For a change let's look at something that can be whipped up in nothing flat.

A quick gift is nice to have around the house. You may have forgotten Aunt Bertha's birthday and when she stops by unexpectedly at teatime on *that* day, you can astound her by handing her this needlecase and thereby amaze her with your forethought and skill!

Green and blue *Pekingese stitch* was used on a gray Jacquard cotton. The edges were *buttonholed* in green. It could be worked in a single strand of wool or two strands of silk depending on the feeling you wish to achieve.

EYEGLASS CASES

If Aunt Bertha needs glasses to find the needles in her gift, you could make her an eyeglass case for Christmas. This one was made from blue cut velvet. Because the blue was so dark, all the stitches were worked in gold Lurex thread.

Straight stitches lend interest to the middle of the flowers and the leaves have *stem stitches* and applied glass beads.

A case may be made in three different ways: using two long rectangles sewn together on three sides; or one very long and narrow piece sewn together on two sides; or a horizontal rectangle sewn together on the bottom and one side.

Whichever way you choose, cut a piece of lining material (nylon, silk, or sateen—but something slippery so that the glasses will slide in and out easily), and meld it to a piece of buckram by basting or gluing. This, in turn, should be placed inside your finished rectangle and the edges are then turned under and *whipped* or *buttonholed* for the finishing touch. Braid can be added for an additional bit of glamour if the material and your desires call for it.

A Stitchery Sampler

Here is another case for someone who likes to experiment with different stitches. This one on chartreuse striped velvet has seventeen different stitches (each one calls for a single strand of wool yarn).

The list shows the exact stitches used.

Cretan
Zigzag chain
Buttonhole
Heavy chain
Wheat ear
Chain
Cross
Twisted chain
Whipped back stitch
Herringbone
Double chain
Darning
Feather
Petal
Stem
Rumanian
Coral

A GEOMETRIC SAMPLE

This material is in direct contrast to the brocade of plate 1 and we show it to illustrate the fact that this embroidery technique can be applied to any and all patterns, be they traditional or ultramodern.

This heavy cotton has a geometric print in a combination of bright glowing oranges and quieter shades of taupe. It is a repeat pattern and would make an extraordinarily handsome bedspread if a vertical panel of squares were embroidered on the top. We show one square worked in eight different stitches, but always using just one strand of wool yarn. Starting at the outside border the four squares, at the corners, were done with a *squared filling* base in dark brown and the *filling stitch* was in white wool.

The small rectangles were formed of parallel rows of *buttonhole stitch* worked diagonally. Two of the largest and airiest rectangles were tied down with a small *straight stitch* about ¼ inch apart.

The heavier-appearing rectangles were composed of *couching*. Two parallel strands of wool were laid down following exactly the direction of the weave in the material. To keep them straight, they were tied down with a small *straight stitch* about ¼ inch apart.

*A variation of
interlocking squares.*

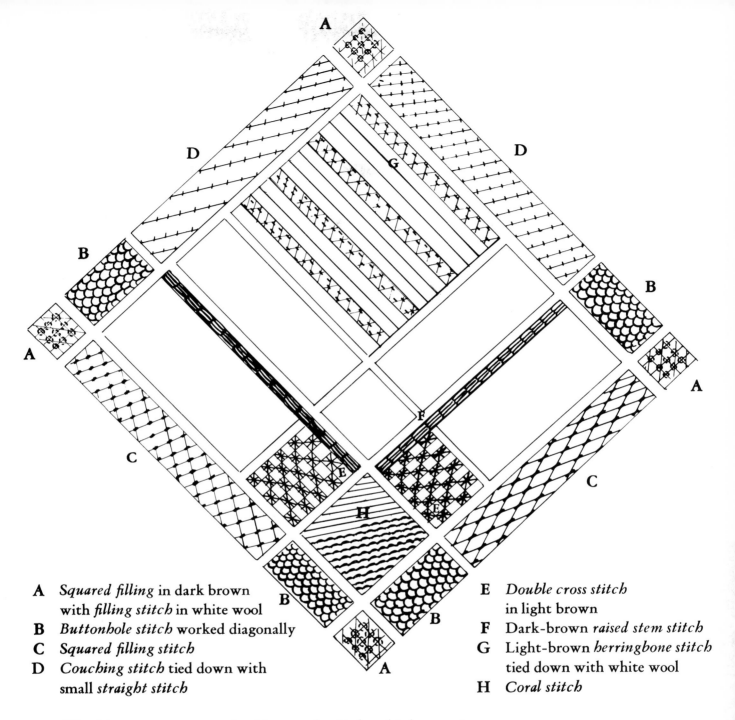

A *Squared filling* in dark brown with *filling stitch* in white wool
B *Buttonhole stitch* worked diagonally
C *Squared filling stitch*
D *Couching stitch* tied down with small *straight stitch*

E *Double cross stitch* in light brown
F Dark-brown *raised stem stitch*
G Light-brown *herringbone stitch* tied down with white wool
H *Coral stitch*

The big square was worked in *coral stitch*, which gave it a very solid effect. The checkerboards were done in a light-brown *double cross stitch*.

The four fatter stripes were made of a combination of light-brown *herringbone* tied down with white yarn. The other two longer and thinner stripes were embroidered in dark-brown *raised stem stitch*.

TRADITIONAL VELVET

Quite often when reminiscing in the attic or cleaning out closets you'll come across a dress that has known better days but that still has hunks of glorious material. Just such a piece was this brilliant blue cut velvet. After embroidering, it could be a panel on an evening skirt or a cover for a jewel box.

The flowers were outlined in light-blue silk *stem stitch* and the leaves were done in a clear-green silk in *chain stitch*.

The root was worked in *coral stitch* and the buds were outlined in *stem* and have *French knots* for accents in two shades of lighter blue.

Certain flowers have circles of bead and baby pearls and some of the leaves have green paillettes. The finished piece is opulent and would make a beautiful evening bag.

This is the same material used in the eyeglass case on page 26 and demonstrates the versatility of most fabrics.

One Material, Two Uses

A STOOL

A stool of this height (14 inches) is a very useful piece of furniture. If firmly built it will serve as a resting spot for you or just for your feet. With the addition of a tray it can do double duty as a coffee table. This stool is covered in a strong yellow cotton matelassé woven in clearly visible chevrons. As the covering would be subject to tension and wear we used a strong wool yarn for the embroidery. Two strands of electric-blue yarn were used for all the vertical lines that bisect the chevrons. These were worked in *heavy chain stitch*.

The diagonal lines were worked in *stem stitch* using a single strand of alternating dusty-pink and grass-green wool—a simple, quick, and effective addition for the chevrons. The stitches were embroidered firmly to avoid any loops that might catch and pull out when in constant use.

A Wastepaper Basket

Wastepaper baskets are a must and one can never have too many. Almost any fabric can be adapted for "slipcovering" either your favorite basket or one that needs quick rejuvenation. Dress materials are perfect for bedrooms and baths but beware of choosing something too light or flimsy, which will pucker when worked (or be murder to mount smoothly). Synthetics behave nicely and come in a fabulous range of patterns and textures. Your living room and library will probably be happier with upholstery fabrics, which tend to be stronger in design and content.

This versatile yellow-and-white cotton is the same as that shown on the preceding stool, only it is inside out! It was so well made that either side could be embroidered, so we chose the lighter side for a change. The finished piece has been done in subtle shades of green but if sewn in bright red or blue it would fit in a child's room to perfection. After the piece was worked the edges were turned over, fastened with pins, and steamed flat. A light coating of rubber cement was applied to the back and it was gently pressed onto the metal basket. The closing was secured temporarily with straight pins and a piece of string was tied around the top and bottom to allow the cement to dry in place securely. After a day, the closing was *whipped* together with thread to tidy up a touch more. The gluing could be omitted but this was a heavy material and we thought it would lie flatter with a bit of help.

The stitchery involved was equally easy. Working from top to bottom:

The first row was done in light green *chain stitch* centered with a single row of dark green *back stitch*.

The wide center band of diagonal bands (forming a chevron) was done in alternating rows of light and dark green *coral stitch*, using two strands of wool.

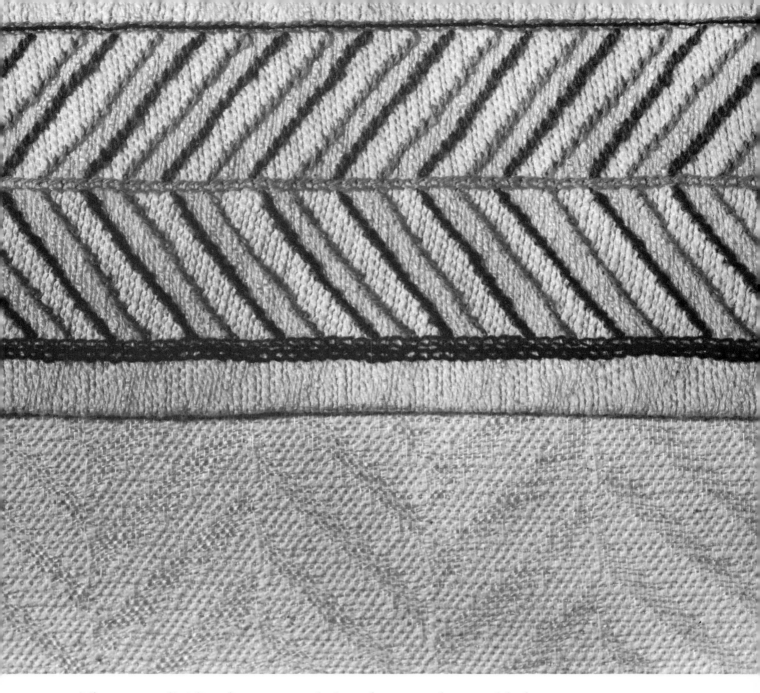

The center dividing line was made by a horizontal row of light green *chain stitch*.

The next two parallel rows were formed by *wide chain stitch* in dark green.

Lastly, there is a single row of *stem stitch* in medium green.

THE VERSATILITY OF BROCADE

A Stool

Brocade offers endless possibilities, from the sublime to the ridiculous. A pincushion or a Louis XV chair would be equally effective using the same fabric.

An all-over repeat pattern of golden chrysanthemums on a white background was used for the stool covering. To complement the yellow flowers, orange-and-brown wool was used to highlight specific blooms. One simple stitch, the *satin*, was used on all flowers; but variety was gained by alternating the combinations of yarn.

This same fabric could be embellished to a delightfully dressier degree by outlining all the flowers and filling in the centers and by using silk thread—or even metallic.

To work this piece we placed the material on the stool and centered the pattern so that the flowers were evenly distributed. We pinned it lightly to the stool and with a single strand of sewing thread we marked each flower to be embroidered and then clearly marked the outside edges. We removed it from the stool and started working from the inside flower outward. This is important if you're not to end up with a handful of heavy fabric (should you start from the outside inward!).

**Three variations
using only two colors
in simple *satin stitch***

As the stool had a slip seat, it was a simple matter to tack the fabric onto the back over the existing cover and screw the seat back into place. All in all, a new, fresh focal point for a room was gained by an expenditure of perhaps three hours' time and two dollars' worth of fabric!

A Pincushion

Using a tiny remnant of the same brocade you can whip up a pincushion for yourself, for Aunt Minnie, or for the church fair. The one shown, again using only the simple *satin stitch*, utilized three shades of blue, and a single strand of yarn. It was cut from two round pieces and one long piece 3 inches wide.

After embroidering, sew the round piece onto the top (from underneath), stuff the cushion with cotton or foam rubber, and *whip* the side piece onto the bottom. A row of *chain stitch* hides the seams and very quickly you have a Christmas gift with the warmest recommendation—your personal touch.

Flowered Satin Pillow

We show another example of the brocade family in plate 2. This apricot satin has an all-over floral pattern of a delicacy that obviously calls for the use of silk threads. The large flowers were outlined in *stem stitch* in a deep shade of apricot. For emphasis smaller flowers were outlined in a red *back stitch*. Centers of the small flowers are comprised of red *French knots*, *stem stitch* outlines flowers and leaves, and they are mostly filled in with *Rumanian stitch*. Some of the smaller areas are completed with the simple *satin stitch*. This also applies to the leaves, which are done in two shades of green. The centers of the large blossoms are done in brown *cross stitch*.

The finished pillow, with its complementary fringe, would add a decorative touch to any bedroom or very formal living room.

Beautiful Bedrooms

HANDSOME HEADBOARD

If your energy knows no bounds, a bedspread and matching headboard would give you a bedroom truly fit for a queen. For lack of time we chose to embroider only the headboard and had the bedspread made up without adornment. Even with one piece done and one to be subsequently worked, in the interim the set is attractive. If the *Farmer's Almanac* predicts enough snowy, wintry days, we might surprise ourselves and finish the bedspread, too. Then we would really have an heirloom for the grandchildren to squabble over. See color plates 10 and 11.

The cotton material was printed in muted gray-greens on an off-white background. It has a slightly ethereal look about it—rather like an ancient Chinese watercolor. Not to disturb the calm color scheme of the flowers, all the embroidery was kept to four shades of soft blue and three shades of delicate green. A single strand of fine wool yarn was used throughout.

All the large flowers—carnations, tulips, and peonies—were outlined in blue *split stitch* and their heavy areas were worked in blue *satin stitch*. Some of the small flowers were outlined in *buttonhole stitch* and had centers of *satin* or *split stitches*, and all were kept in the blue family of yarns.

The stems and leaves were outlined either in *chain* or *twisted chain* in one of the three shades of green. A much more vibrant effect would have resulted from the use of louder colors, but for a bedroom we opted for tranquillity.

38

The brass headboard had an indented area, which was uncomfortable and caused the pillows to be totally uncooperative and fall down the crack. We bought a piece of ⅜-inch plywood, cut it to fit, padded it with cotton batting, and covered it with muslin. Our embroidered cotton fitted on top of this and was simply tacked over and onto the back; and the finished product was pushed into the frame (exactly like the slip seat of a chair). The result is not only aesthetic, it's extremely comfortable, and we heartily recommend the entire project.

BEDSPREADS FROM FASCINATING FABRICS

The wealth of ideas for bedspreads is staggering. Faced with hundreds of chintzes, linens, and various other fabrics was like eating peanuts—we couldn't stop.

With this new decorating concept in mind we saw all the materials in a new light. We didn't admire them because they were pink or green, but because of their slumbering personalities and what we could do to emphasize their beauty.

The unmounted samples that we show in plates 6, 7, 8, and 9 were left that way deliberately. There are so many interesting cotton, cretonne, linen, woven, printed, flat, and bumpy fabrics available that it was almost impossible to narrow the field to the few shown in this book. Therefore, we have tried to give diverse designs that might suggest specific uses to the reader. For example, the white linen shown in plate 8 has an extremely powerful pattern printed in charcoal gray. It would make a handsome accent pillow. Or perhaps you have an old side chair that is crying out for a coat of charcoal-gray paint and that would then happily welcome this smashing pink embroidery on its slip seat. If not an heirloom, it would at least be a conversation piece!

So, with these samples as guides, browse around your local mill-end shops and see what your imagination says to you. You may feel like merely doing a small pillow. On the other hand, your energy may be riding high and Grandma's Victorian love seat could well be in for a face-lift with this new and exciting technique.

Whichever it is—have fun. This is not an exercise in endurance —it is more a labor of love.

Yellow Chintz

A yellow chintz with mouth-watering strawberries and flowers in an all-over design may be seen in plate 9.

The strawberries are partially outlined in two parallel rows of stem stitch using dark-red cotton thread. The white flowers are *buttonholed*. The shading on the leaves is more intricate and varies from *running stitches* made with one strand of dark-green wool to a single-strand *double chain* for the veins and stems.

The darker-green stems are in *double chain* and the light-green stems are in *herringbone*.

Celadon and Pink Chintz

The floral chintz in plate 7 with massed flowers in white and pink would make a beautiful bedspread—or if you felt a little less ambitious, it would make up into a lovely pillow. A single strand of wool yarn was used throughout and to start with we did the flowers and buds in dusty pink and a deeper shade of rose using the *stem stitch*. The thin rows are in *chain stitch* and the thicker ones called for *herringbone stitch*. These alternated in green and pink.

A row of *herringbone* also outlined the buds. The centers of the flowers were accented with green *satin stitch*.

The green leaves were outlined in a lighter-green *buttonhole stitch* and the veins were picked out in a dark-green *coral stitch*.

The white flowers, which have pink accents, are composed of alternating *French knots* and *chain stitch*. The *French knots* are the only stitches calling for two strands of yarn as a single strand makes an anemic knot!

Another batch of *French knots* in two shades of lightish green enlivens the solid pink areas.

This was a smoothly woven chintz and a joy to work on. It could have more or less embroidery depending on its designated use in your room. Whether it would be "more" or "less," the results would be equally gratifying.

Gray and Gold Pattern

The floral chintz in plate 6 has such a busy design that it called for very little embellishment. If you slipcovered a chair in this chintz and then made up a matching pillow with the design embroidered as we show it, you would have a terrific duo.

The overall color scheme was gray and yellow and the pattern a bit on the fussy side, so it needed only "accenting" and not "covering." All the insides of the embroidered flowers were done in *satin stitch* using a single strand of light-brown wool.

The heavily worked leaves have rose-colored veins in *coral stitch* with side veins in a light-appearing *stem stitch*.

The more delicate leaves have veins in *coral stitch* using a single strand of yarn in a soft shade of green.

VARIATIONS ON A THEME

A Box

Here we show two completely different ready-made articles utilizing the same dotted fabric. They are classic examples of how the total effect can be so easily changed by using diverse groupings of stitches. The pale-blue satin had tiny white dots marching up and down with beautiful precision. It reminded us of that children's drawing puzzle called "follow-the-dots." So, we traveled the dots horizontally, vertically, and diagonally with rows of *couching* in twelve different shades of silk thread. Six strands of each color were used to make it heavy enough, and each row ends with a *paillette* for an exclamation point.

The cover could be changed for the seasons as the top of the box was made for simple insertions. The box was obtained from a needle-craft shop.

A Desk Blotter

The blotter has slipcovered ends of the same dotted satin, but in a slightly darker shade of blue. To make it appear less fragile, we used wool yarns instead of silk. The outside borders were embroidered in two tones of green in a *detached zigzag stitch* using two strands of wool in each shade. The central column is composed of *fly stitches* in the lighter green with centers of chartreuse *French knots* for added interest. It was quite easy to make the straight lines by just following the dots. Almost any stitches can be used on a fabric like this and the pertinent decision is rather whether you use silk or wool for your embroidery.

Tremendous Trifles

MATCHBOXES

You may think we've chosen too many large pieces and that they are too challenging. If your idea of heaven is to run up something in an hour or so, we have just the answer to your prayers.

Color plate 12 shows three variations on a matchbox theme. All were made quickly and easily from a sample book of damask fabrics having diamond patterns.

The rust cover has an interlocking diamond pattern in two complementary colors of silk thread. Three strands were used in *double chain stitch.*

The blue satiny damask has a repeat pattern of *feather-stitched* diamonds using three strands of pale-pink silk thread. An *elongated cross stitch* in maroon silk was placed in the middle of each diamond and tied down with two small *parallel stitches.*

The beige cover already looked quilted and took very little embellishing to finish it off. The blue "snowflake" motifs are a variation of the *double cross stitch*, which was tied down with one stitch in the center. The green diamonds were worked in *stem.* All used one single strand of wool yarn.

The mounting is usually not a problem. We happened to have an old leather box and we used it for the blue case. This fabric had pinked edges, which didn't seem inclined to ravel, so we simply used rubber cement to attach our handiwork on the top, after stitching down the folded-over ends so that the case slid into them firmly.

44

In the case of the rust-and-beige covers, we turned over the outer edges and basted them down, then pressed them to get a clean-cut knife edge. We then glued them to the box. If you have enough fabric, it is nice also to cover the ends.

TELEPHONE-BOOK COVER

Do you need a telephone-book cover for a teenager or a sun room or some spot that calls for gaiety? Turn to plate 14.

We found a simple cotton with startling flowers in the brightest of colors. The orange and yellow blossoms were worked in *Rumanian stitch* using a single strand of wool.

The two shades of pink and rose are *satin stitch* and the "dots" inside the flowers are *detached chain stitch*.

The cover was purchased ready-made, the material cut to fit, and then worked. After finishing and pressing it, a small layer of cotton was laid onto the cover (to give added "puffiness" to the flowers) and then rubber cement was applied around the edges before they were pushed under the frames. They were pushed under with a blunt nail file. Being a lightweight cotton, it caused some frustration in the mounting process. It's been ironed three times and still looks mussed up, for which we apologize. To avoid this pitfall, we suggest that you use a firmer fabric.

FOLDING JEWEL CASE

The traveling jewel case shown in plate 18 is readily found in any notions department of a dry-goods store. We simply *whipped* the finished cotton brocade over the existing fabric—this makes it easily removable for cleaning. This same procedure would apply to cases for cosmetics or sewing or any other necessary "notions."

The top flowers were worked in two shades of rose using a single strand of wool in a *twisted chain stitch.* The centers are brown *satin stitch.* The stems were formed by the *Cretan stitch* in green wool.

Two shades of green worked in *burden stitch* made the central motif most interesting. The pendulous bulblike pods with turned-up ends like Turkish slippers are in purple *threaded chain.*

The two bottom red blossoms were *couched* with added *back stitches.* The bottom leaves consist of two shades of green in *twisted chain* filled with *feather stitch*—all were worked with a single strand of wool yarn.

To simplify the understanding of the embroidery, study the tracing diagram.

A   *Satin stitch*
B   *Burden stitch*
C   *Twisted chain stitch*
D   *Cretan stitch*
E   *Threaded chain stitch*
F   *Feather stitch*
G   *Couching with back stitch*

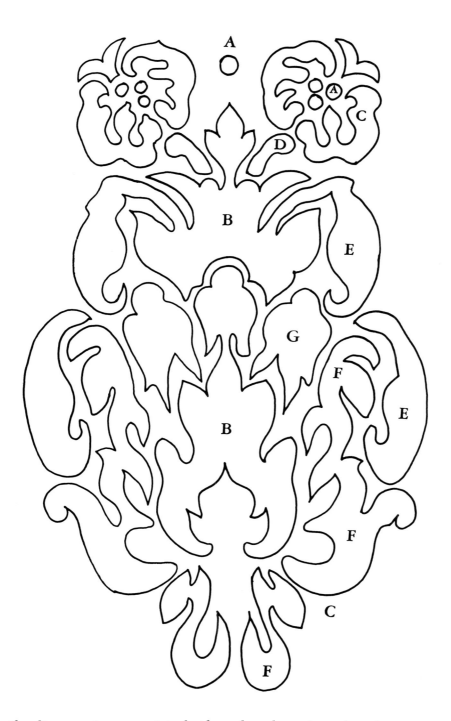

As the diagram is symmetrical, the colors have been keyed on one side only.

Enhancing Unusual Motifs

ONE OF THE JOYS of traveling lies in finding and bringing home indigenous souvenirs. With this new embroidery hobby in mind you'll look at local costumes and textiles with a different eye. On a recent trip to New Mexico the distinctive flavor of Indian artwork compelled us to buy this apron and these two dresses. The designs were simple, yet very strong, and in most cases only one or two colors were used. A small amount of embroidery merely heightened an already attractive arrangement of forms, but at the same time gave each garment a personalized touch.

ZUNI APRON

The apron was made of a hand-woven cotton and is predominantly black and white. With the addition of only two colors and by using only three different stitches, this special souvenir became a more handsome reminder of our visit to Indian country.

From left to right the stitches are as follows:

The red was done in *Cretan stitch*

Blue in *stem stitch*

Red in *chain stitch*

Blue in *Cretan stitch*

Another blue in *chain*

These were followed by two more red in *Cretan* and lastly two more blue in *Cretan*.

Because it's impossible to tell the colors from a black-and-white photograph, we show a diagram with the colors keyed.

48

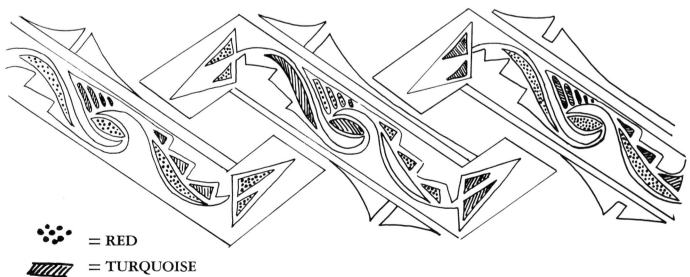

= RED

= TURQUOISE

WHITE SHEATH WITH BORDER

An old ghost town in the mountains of Santa Fe County has been rediscovered and resurrected. Craft shops and galleries have opened up and the local artists are flocking in with the fruits of their labors. This long, white cotton dress has a stark design painted around the hem in chocolate brown. Because of the thickness of the paint, it was only possible to use a limited number of stitches—as it was, we had a hard time getting the needle in and out. But we thought it worth the effort and softened the overall effect with the addition of turquoise over-embroidery. To cover the paint thoroughly, three strands of turquoise mercerized floss were used. The top circles were done in a tight *Rumanian stitch* and the vertical accents called for the use of *tied-down herringbone stitches.*

The dress screams for accessorizing. Depending on whatever color embroidery you team with the brown design, you can be frivolous or monastically severe. An Indian belt of silver and turquoise would be beautiful with our chosen combination. This particular combination of blue and brown seemed typically Southwestern. Or, leaving the dark brown to its already designated prominence, you might add a lighter shade of beige or rust embroidery. Then a necklace of heavy white beads might be your preference to complete your outfit. Whatever you choose, you can look at it in later years and remember your trip and the happy time you had browsing in unknown territory.

As the dress was totally unadorned except for the border we show only that part of the garment.

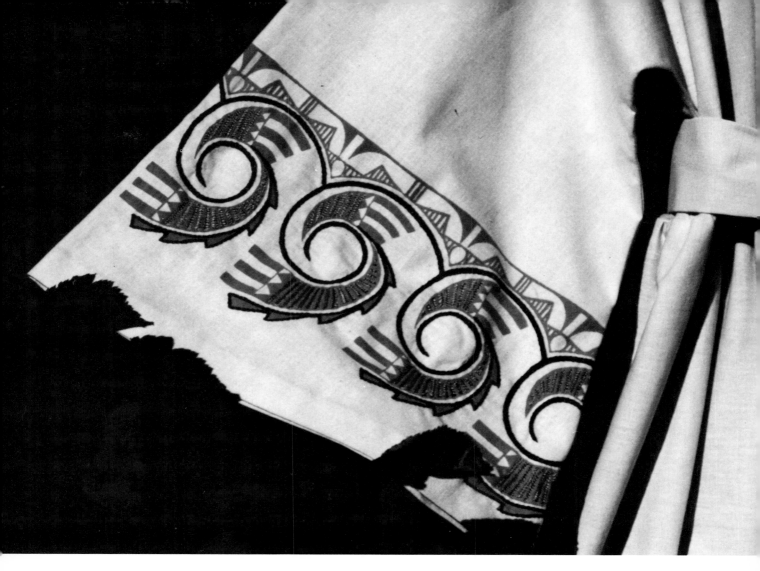

HAND-WOVEN DRESS

From New Mexico also came this Taos gown of locally loomed chartreuse cotton. The print was hand-screened with a design inspired by the walls of a Zuni pueblo. The inner design, which was printed in a vibrant shade of rust, had yellow open lines which we filled in with three strands of turquoise embroidery threads in the *herringbone stitch*.

The remaining circles were worked in a *double chain stitch* using three strands of dark-brown floss. The jagged leaflike design was also worked in the same dark brown, but in a *single chain stitch*. The entire dress may be seen in color in plate 28.

A SUPER SWEATER

Still on the subject of clothing, but switching to an entirely different type of attire, we're showing a typical all-American sweater.

For instant success take one solid-color shift and add this machine-made white sweater. We added the navy-blue medallions and outlined them in green following the design in the sweater. Presto—an ensemble and one versatile enough to wear traveling. This is a recipe for simple chic which is sometimes called "expensive simplicity." In our case it's "inexpensive simplicity," as nearly everyone has a simple plain dress and the market is flooded with attractive ready-made sweaters. The one we chose was an acrylic, so we purchased one small ball of navy-blue synthetic wool. We experimented with straight pins and decided upon the groupings on the shoulder and the sleeves and in a straight line parallel to the borders.

Five parallel vertical lines, graduating upward in length from the outside, were tied down with a *cross stitch*, which in turn was tied down with another *cross stitch*. This is a "made-up" stitch and is simply a combination of *satin* and *cross stitches*. Then it was a simple matter to run a single full-strength strand of green D.M.C. floss (six threads) around the outside under and over the existing sweater stitches. Any color combination will work and even the reverse of ours would be effective—that is, if you had a white dress you could have a blue sweater with white medallions.

The Wonderful World of Gingham

FOR A COMPLETE CHANGE OF PACE we're showing a series of articles made of gingham. You don't even have to follow the lines or think about intricate shading—all you have to do is to be able to count!

The dictionary calls gingham "a firm cotton fabric yarn-dyed and woven in solid colors: stripes or checks." We have used both cotton and polyester gingham, the former for a child's outfit and the latter for some aprons. Whichever you choose, it's a simple matter to attach your material to the board with short pieces of masking tape, which readily peel off when you've finished marking the design. A soft No. 2 pencil should be used to make slight dots on the squares to be embroidered. If you have a large design utilizing two shades of yarn or floss, make dots for one shade and dashes for the other. This way, when the hoop is in place and you can't see all of the design, you will not be confused as to the proper placement of either colored stitch.

MOTIFS ON GRAPHS

To simplify your reproduction problems, we show tracing diagrams and graphs. Graphs are very explicit and leave little room for error. It is also fun to experiment on graph paper with free-form "doodling." You may be amazed to find that a certain series of circles might well translate into a smashing design. The graphs shown on the next few pages all started out life in doodling form—rectangles and squares were mere squiggles on the pad until one seemed just right. Then it was carefully worked out by counting the squares on the graph. All, except the one here were then

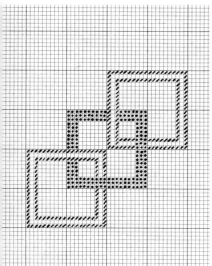

embroidered on gingham and are shown in the photographs. The unworked graph was included to show one of a possible hundred "variations on an entwined square theme." We used only two different colors and only *cross stitch* and *tied-down cross stitch* for the embroidery. Gingham doesn't have a very long life and therefore it seemed silly to get very complicated in its treatment.

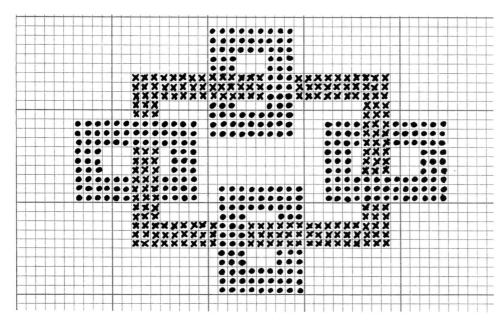

X = BLUE
0 = WHITE

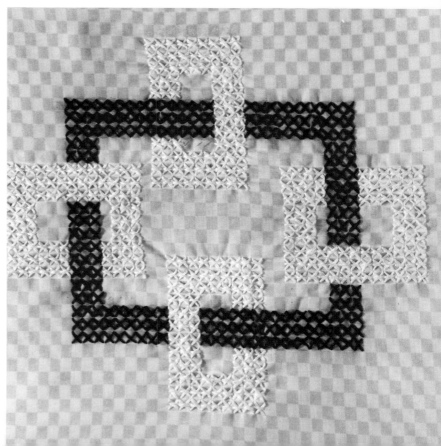

Scallop Shell

The shell called for the most concentration. We first sketched it lightly on the graph paper, then started at the top and marked the center section, diminishing the squares down to the point at the bottom. Each side followed (with more mathematics than artistry involved). The finished scallop shell might not please Botticelli, but it certainly looks like a shell and that's all we desired. Two shades of red and one of pink delineated the sections, and a few stitches in white accented the sides. Four strands of mercerized cotton floss were used in the basic *cross stitch*. This motif would be beguiling on the little green sunsuit shown in plate 19.

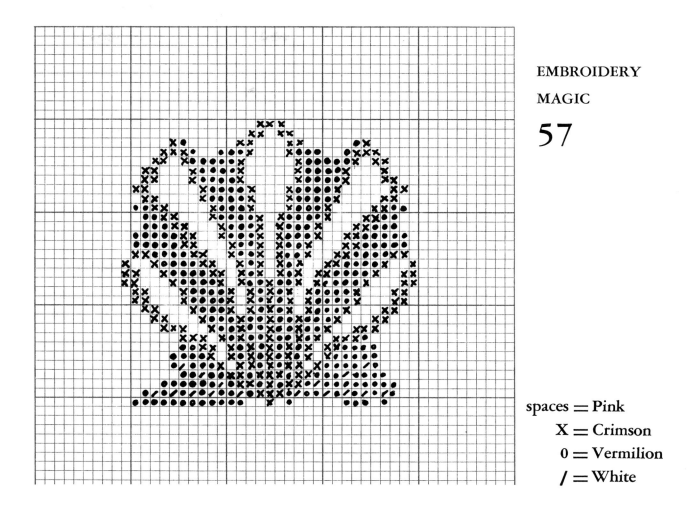

spaces = Pink

X = Crimson

0 = Vermilion

/ = White

APRONS

An apron is forever. Babies start off with abbreviated aprons under chins as bibs. Little girls graduate to wearing a pinafore-type apron to save spoiling their party dresses, and big girls end up sporting aprons to avoid soiling their clothes in the kitchen. One way or another the female of the species spends a great deal of her time in an apron and therefore you can never have too many.

An Apron with Wings

Here we show a navy-blue gingham apron of cotton. The design was first worked out on graph paper to make sure that each section was evenly and correctly spaced. Other "wings" might be added for a more intricate design, which would give the overall effect of a snowflake. The material was laid out flat upon the work table and the size decided upon. This measured 23 x 23 inches before hemming. We folded the fabric in half to find the exact center, marked it with a pin, and then after unfolding it we taped it to the board.

After allowing for 3 inches at the top for turning over the waistband, we centered the graph on the fabric. It looked right, so we started lightly marking the center axis and worked outward from there with geometric precision. We used a No. 2 pencil to mark the material lightly and made "X's" for the white stitches and "O's" for the navy blue. We found it easier to work outward from the center, doing the corresponding stitch marks for each "petal" or wing. As the design grew larger, it was easier to check and make sure that all four arms were growing in unison. When the marking was finished we used a hoop to hold this light fabric firmly in place, doing two arms at a time.

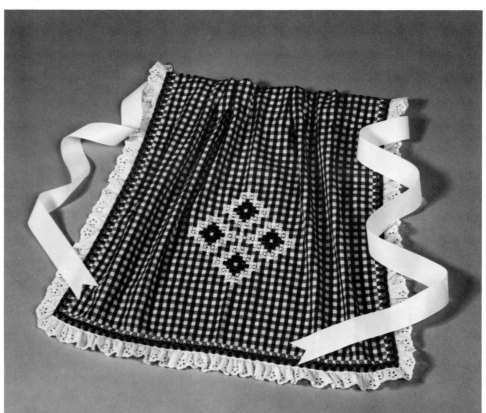

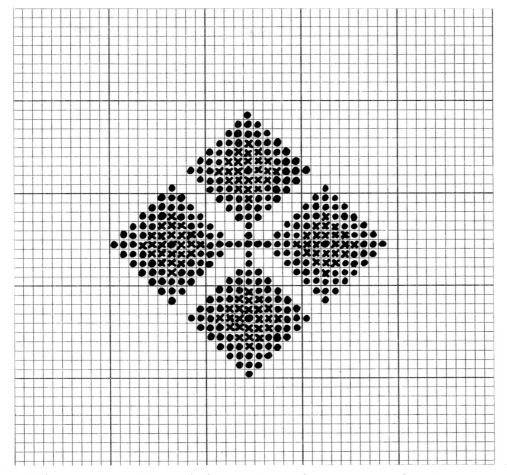

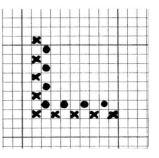

0 = WHITE
X = NAVY BLUE

BORDER

The outer portions of the sections, three squares deep in most cases, were marked in a *double cross stitch* using six strands of white embroidery floss (commonly called D.M.C.). The exact center square was also done in white, and the interim spaces were worked in navy blue. When the design was finished (and it went very, very quickly) we turned under the edges of our apron-to-be and added white eyelet embroidery to brighten up the navy gingham. For an added fillip we did two parallel rows of *double cross stitch* with one in navy blue and the other in white, still using six strands of floss. After sewing down the waistband we ran 2 yards of white grosgrain ribbon through it and were ready for any superior KP duty.

An Apron with Daisies

Here's another apron which is soft and feminine and very practical. You can dump it in the kitchen sink and drip-dry it, as it's made of pure polyester. We bought a yard (too much) and laid it flat on the work table. Armed with a handful of straight pins we marked groupings of the same flowers. When we were finished, the resulting design turned out to be mathematically even—proving that old adage about "not being able to fool the naked eye."

The inner flowers were worked in *detached chain* (sometimes known as *lazy-daisy stitch*) using six strands of D.M.C. white floss. In the center of each "petal" we added a *straight stitch* to give the flower more body. The exact center is a medium blue *French knot* (again using six strands because it made a nice fat knot even though it was a bit of a tug to get it through the fabric). The darker flowers are made of two shades of blue—each shade being considerably darker than the pale blue of the background. *Detached chain* (*lazy-daisy stitches*) in the lighter blue formed the petals, and again they were filled in with a single *straight stitch*, but this time in a very dark blue using six strands of floss. The exact center of these blue flowers is a fat *French knot* for contrast.

We then roll-hemmed the two sides and the bottom and turned over the top to make a drawstring channel for the sash. Three-quarters of a yard of material would have been sufficient, as we had to cut off at least 5 inches after turning over the top of the apron. For a frothy finishing touch, we whipped on a border of white ready-made eyelet embroidery. When that was done, the leftover piece was utilized by cutting it in half and sewing a 12-inch length of elastic to the two inner ends. When inserted into the drawstring channel, the elastic won't show and will serve to gather the waistband nicely, leaving the eyelet for the tie part of the belt. Only a yard of embroidery trim was needed because of the invisible insertion. So don your apron and off you go to the party (via the kitchen!).

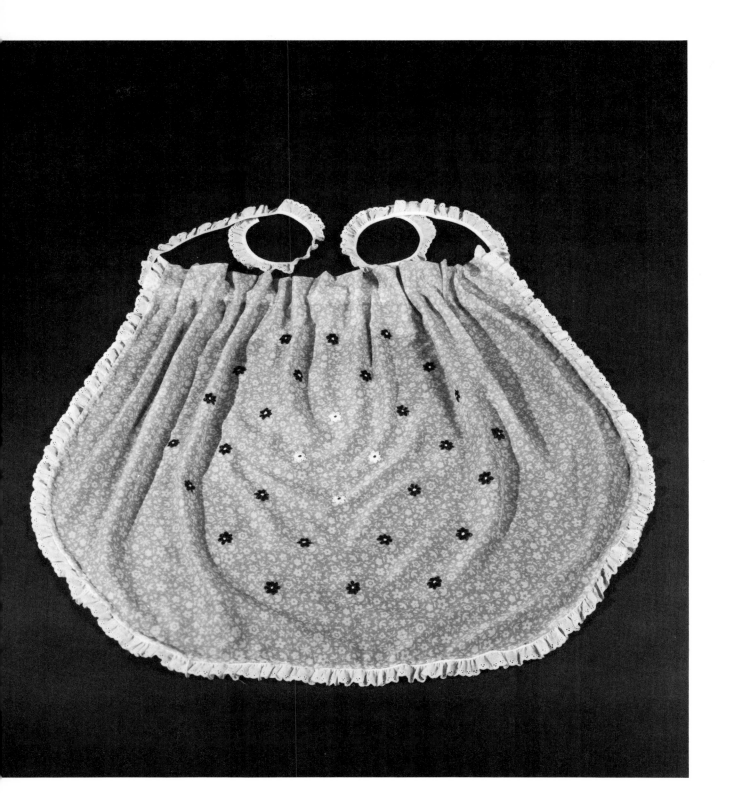

Apron with a Checked Border

An apron, involving very little work, is a green-and-white checked gingham cotton with stitching in plum and yellow.

The outlines and centers are *cross stitched* in three rows of plum cotton using two strands. The fill-in patterns are yellow *cross stitches* with four radiating *straight stitches* in plum. This was done on the hem and on the pocket, but could have been done on the body of the apron by following the squares in a hexagonal form or at random.

WASTEPAPER BASKET

Any simple material will glamorize a plain metal basket and tie it into the color scheme of your bedroom. This common gingham presented endless variations, but quite often the simplest proves to be the best.

By holding the fabric against the basket the shape and size were marked with pins and the centers of front and back marked with small safety pins.

The pattern is done in dark-blue single-strand wool yarn. Starting at the top you have a row of *chain stitch* in blue, a row of *wheat ear* in green, and another row of *chain* in blue. Next a "V" is formed by dark-blue *cross stitches* tied down in the center. Four *detached chain stitches* radiate from the center of the cross.

The central cross was formed by a *squared filling* in emerald green, tied down with light blue. In the center motifs (and at the end of the cross between the bars) are nine *French knots* in dark blue.

To mount it, pin the material around the basket for exact fit. Then iron the edges flat and apply rubber cement lightly to the basket (making sure it is thick enough to hold, but not so heavy that it will soak through the fabric).

Where the ends overlap, cement the two edges and lightly pin them flat. Using sewing thread wrap the entire basket in a light web of thread. This keeps the fabric taut and allows the cement to dry without the seams popping open in any spots. Using rubber cement will also allow you to remove the fabric for cleaning.

Imaginative Inserts
for Ready-Mades

Gift shops, craft shops, and needlework emporiums abound in already assembled articles that need only a little attention to turn them into smashing and personalized gifts.

ICE BUCKET WITH KEY DESIGN

The dusty old-time knitting shop (complete with a live cat snoozing in a basket of wool in the window) seems to have gone the way of the horse and buggy. Today's needlework boutiques sell everything from petit-point picture frames to bargello backgammon boards. They also have a fantastic range of gifts to adorn people or homes. This ice bucket was just such an appealing item. We discarded the accompanying canvas and chose a piece of Jacquard yellow cotton woven in a mathematically precise pattern. The so-called "key" design was worked in alternating teal-blue and brown motifs. The thin rows are made of *split stitch* and the thicker ones have two parallel rows of the same. This is a pleasing repeat pattern, which could be greatly varied by the addition of more colors or different stitches. In fact, the more, the merrier!

64

A paper pattern was cut to fit the inside of the bucket, as it was slightly rounded. Then a Pellon pattern was cut from it and glued (with rubber cement) onto the back of the finished piece. The edges were ironed down and the whole thing slipped between the outside of the bucket and the provided ice liner. These buckets come with mounting directions and are truly simple to put together. Depending on your room's decor you could choose from dozens of fabrics. However, for the ease of mounting we suggest chintz in cotton or linen. Anything bulky will not have a tidy look when mounted.

A WALL SCONCE

Needlework shops and mail-order stitchery catalogs offer a wide choice of objects that may be adapted to this new hobby. A case in point is this candleholder. If you live at the Arctic Circle and have to spend the greater part of the year indoors, you might want to do a time-consuming piece of twenty-to-the-inch petit-point canvas for your insertion. If, however, you are a housewife who cooks, cleans, chauffeurs, P.T.A.s, goes to classes, etc., you might settle for this yellow-and-white textured cotton. It is woven in a clearly visible pattern of diamonds and stripes.

The embroidery directions are as follows: looking from left to right (and using only one strand of wool yarn) work the outside column in blue using the *straight stitch*.

Next comes a column of red *buttonhole* worked on a slant. Four blue diamonds follow in *burden stitch*. The rows of *laid stitches*, which run horizontally, are deep fuchsia and their vertical *straight stitches* are blue. The four maroon diamonds are composed of *squared filling* with the initial stitches being done in fuchsia and the secondary ones in blue.

The directions for mounting the finished insertion usually come with the product and are very easy to comprehend.

A TRAY

The tray in plate 22 has a readily accessible section for the insertion of a piece of needlepoint, bargello, or embroidery. We found an attractive chintz in a fresh, up-to-date combination of blues and greens. The design being already pleasing, it called for only a small amount of embellishment and in no time at all it was worked, ironed, and mounted under the glass. Only two different stitches were used and the work went very quickly, although the finished piece belies the ease of execution.

The flowers and leaves have their veins outlined in *split stitch* using a single strand of dark-green wool. Pale-blue *split stitches* were used for lighter accents. The centers of the flowers were adorned with *French knots* using two strands of wool yarn in two different shades of green. The *French knots* in the strawberries were done in dark green in order to have a strong contrast to the printed pink of the fruit. The tray came painted a gay green and this chintz with its clear, natural colors was a perfect match. The finished piece is protected by the glass and may be removed at any time for pressing. When you are inserting a fabric into a tray, an ice bucket, or a magazine rack (where it must lie smoothly under glass or plastic) it is best to choose a lightweight but firm material such as chintz or tightly woven cotton and synthetics. A heavy fabric will present problems when you have to turn the edges under for mounting and the resulting bulkiness will make it untidy-looking and it will be very difficult to handle.

If you've found a thickly woven fabric that enchants you above all others, and you feel you *must* use it (even though turning the edges under will be nearly impossible), try this: use pinking shears on the edges—providing the fabric is woven tightly enough not to ravel. Another solution, to avoid the turning-the-edge-under doldrums, is to cut the edges very carefully and evenly and then use a close-together *buttonhole stitch* as a binding. Before trying this, cut off a tiny piece and experiment to see if it frays. Sometimes if the material is truly opaque, you can put a thin strip of masking tape on the back and *buttonhole* right over this resulting firm double layer. Thin fabrics are the easiest, as they may simply be turned over and ironed flat and the covering glass holds them in place.

DIAMONDS AND DAISIES

By now you may want to see something quick and easy. This box is available from needlework shops and we simply removed the canvas provided and mounted a small piece of woolen brocade in a diamond pattern.

Before inserting, it was worked as follows: Each diamond has a flower in the center. The flowers are worked in *satin stitch* and the edge of the diamond is outlined with a *buttonhole stitch*.

The backgrounds of the remaining diamonds are filled in with *stem stitch* with the flowers left plain—except for a glass "fake jewel" in each center. They are sewn down and rimmed with *stem stitch*.

Perfect Presents

TABLE TALK

Table mats are in the market in bewildering profusion. We chose a yellow-and-white synthetic straw in an old-fashioned gingham pattern and worked two for the sake of variety.

Using cotton thread (for ease in washing) we did the border in a red *satin stitch*. All the squares were done in *eye stitch*. (We often wonder where they got the names for some of the stitches.)

The second mat is exactly the same, but showing a different treatment. The outside border consists of four parallel rows of *running stitch*. Next inside row is *double cross stitch*. The inside flowers are composed of *back stitch* with a *cross stitch* in each center. Six strands of red cotton thread were used in all cases.

BLANKET FOR A BABY

Babies' and children's clothing and accessories have universal appeal. Baby blankets are always useful gifts and would be lovely examples of your "caring."

We found an enchanting hand-woven one in a soft sea green and gave it royal-blue accents by easily following the actual weave. The pattern was worked out first on tracing paper and it was decided that the very loose weave of the blanket called for "*pulled-work stitches*. Pulled stitches are those which are more tightly worked to create an openwork pattern.

The center medallion is in *eye stitch* with an outer frame in *satin stitch*. The four corners are *satin stitch* with a *double cross stitch* in each center. The four oblongs are composed of rows of *raised diagonal band*.

Because a baby blanket should be washable, a synthetic yarn was used for the embroidery. In order to retain the airy feeling of the blanket, a single strand was used in the simple stitches.

A GLAMOROUS TOWEL

Another small item with a ginghamlike air is actually made of green-and-white terry cloth. Because of the depth of the pile on this towel, it was necessary to use four strands of cotton floss. The stitches show up well when done in a complementary shade of forest green. A set of towels, enlivened with embroidery, would make a very welcome engagement or wedding present and yet the monetary outlay wouldn't be frightening.

Working from the bottom left upward by rows, we did the border in *herringbone stitch*. Then rows one and four were worked in *wheat ear* and rows two and three are *buttonhole* (worked diagonally).

The second grouping of rows was even simpler. Rows one, three, and five were done in *zigzag chain* and rows two and four are *diagonal buttonhole*.

Results good; effort minimal.

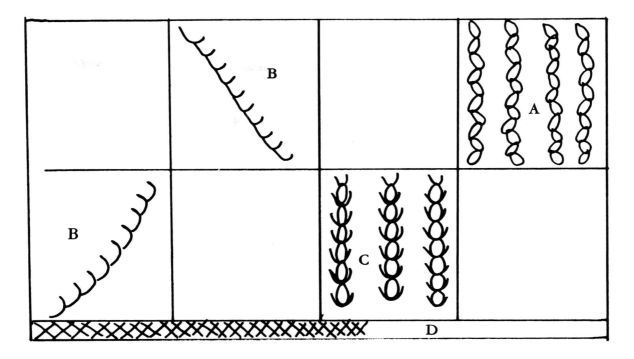

A *Zigzag chain stitch*
B Diagonally worked *buttonhole stitch*
C *Wheat-ear stitch*
D *Herringbone stitch*

GIRL'S SUNSUIT

Whether you are a new mother or a doting grandma, it's always fun to buy children's clothes. The misguided days of Little Lord Fauntleroy's velvet suits have fortunately passed into folklore and today's children are comfortably and happily dressed in "wash and wear." (See plate 19.)

This sunsuit in pale-green-and-white gingham was purchased in a chain store for less than three dollars. Thirty minutes after reaching home, it had been made "Jane's very own" by the easy addition of her name. It was embroidered with six strands of dark-green mercerized cotton in a *tied-down cross stitch*—a stitch that will survive thousands of trips to the washing machine. The graph shows how easily "JANE" may be worked—Cleopatra or Mehitabel would take a little longer.

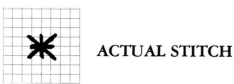 **ACTUAL STITCH**

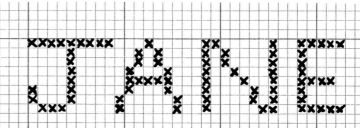

BOY'S SUNSUIT

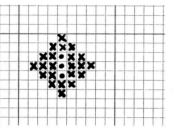

X = GREEN
0 = WHITE

For the male of the family (junior grade) we found a companion sunsuit of blue-and-white stripes. We marked with small safety pins the areas needing a "lift" and embroidered an easy motif using apple green and pure white mercerized cotton thread. The center bar is in six strands of white in *satin stitch* and the surrounding stitches were done in light-green *tied-down cross stitches*. An embroidery hoop was a necessity, as the lightweight knit fabric slithered all over the place. Also, it was a bit of a chore placing the stitches correctly without benefit of the vertical guidelines (which we'd become used to in the gingham fabrics). (See plate 19.)

Names, nicknames, or team names could also be done on a stripe like this—it's purely a matter of preference and patience.

A SCARF

Scarves may be purchased ready-made (as this was) or made up from remnants of some material that just plain appeals to you. This simple silk is quick, easy, and useful for myriad occasions. If you have a yen to be glamorous, try a few yards of brocade and work the flowers in gold or silver threads for a truly fantastic evening shawl. Buy enough fabric to line your finished piece so that you won't get scratched by the metallic thread—or line it in a complementary shade of light silk.

Our navy-blue-and-white example has the embroidery done in American-beauty red cotton and it enlivens it no end.

The bottom row, from left to right, has alternating rectangles of *chain* and *Cretan stitches*.

The second row has four rectangles done in *stem stitch*.

The third row is embroidered in *wheat ear* and *stem stitches*. (See diagram for clarification.)

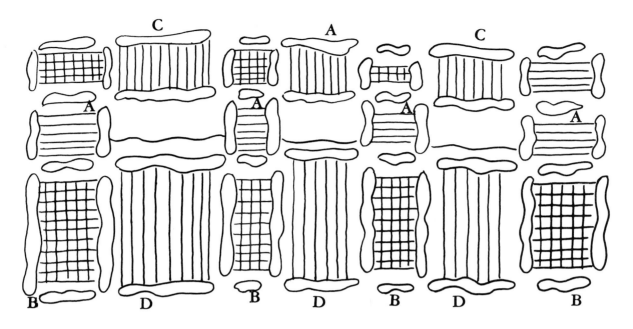

A   *Stem stitch*
B   *Chain stitch*
C   *Wheat-ear stitch*
D   *Cretan stitch*

PLAYING-CARD CASE

Another gift item readily found in department stores and needle-work shops is this lucite case for playing cards. The top calls for a simple insertion of any type of material. We chose a beige cotton chintz with free-form blue-and-green flowers printed on it.

All the flowers were embroidered in *Rumanian stitch* in varying shades of blue wool yarn using a single strand.

The large central flower has a chartreuse silk *spiderweb* and the circles are also *outlined* in chartreuse silk in the *stem stitch*.

All leaves and stems were done in *herringbone* in green. It is interesting to note how the closely worked Rumanian stitch looks so very different from the loosely embroidered version of the same stitch.

MOIRÉ BOOK COVER

As a material, moiré, or watered silk, lends itself to a thousand uses, but to embellish it demands more imagination.

The patterns are very open and ethereal and they don't have the clearly defined shapes of brocades or chintz or gingham. It presents a real challenge and the finished gift will truly be one of a kind.

This rust cotton moiré book cover was worked in single-strand wool in three shades of green and three of rust. All the outlines were done in *coral stitch*. If the yarn is very thin, it would be advantageous to use two strands for the *coral stitch* to make it more prominent. The heavier, long sections are *herringbone tied down*. The smaller areas were filled in with either *feather* or *satin stitches*.

Enhancing Ready-Mades

A DECORATED JEWEL BOX

An example of working on an already finished article is the jewel box shown in plate 13. It is Thai silk striped in various shades of red and fuchsia. Pretty, but unexciting.

We turned it into a queenly jewel case by the simple addition of rows of *chain stitch* worked with a single strand of silver metallic thread. We counted the stripes and worked every other one until reaching the center, where two were worked next to each other to make the remainder come out evenly. As no knots could be made, the threaded needle was inserted one-third of the way down from the top where the first stitch would occur. As the chain progressed downward, it caught the "starting" thread underneath and anchored it. When we reached the bottom, we simply turned around and worked upward. This down-and-up-and-down-again method soon had the top quickly and easily covered. To finish off the thread, we ran it under the finished chain for at least 2 inches and cut off the end close to the surface. For further glamorizing, two diagonal rows were stitched and, where they met in the middle, an amethyst crystal pin was securely placed. A final touch was the row of *chain* around the edge of the lid, and with a minimum of effort we had turned a utilitarian box into a tiny treasure house for our favorite jewels.

78

STRAW HAT

If it's a warm day, slip on this straw hat. A *back stitch* is worked following the diagonal of the weave.

It is worked in single-strand wool in yellow, blues, pink, and green. The trim on the brim is *buttonhole*. The band around the crown consists of single strands of each of the colored yarns twisted together in rope fashion and then ending in a multicolored tassel. The band is fastened at each diagonal intersection with a *straight stitch* in the matching yarn.

AN ADAPTABLE BELT

A lady's belt in yellow string has its edges *whipped* in green with red *cross stitches* below.

The center panel has two close-together rows of blue cotton and gold metallic Christmas string just woven in and out like a running stitch.

The "jewels" have holes on either side and are sewn onto the belt with thread that matches the stones.

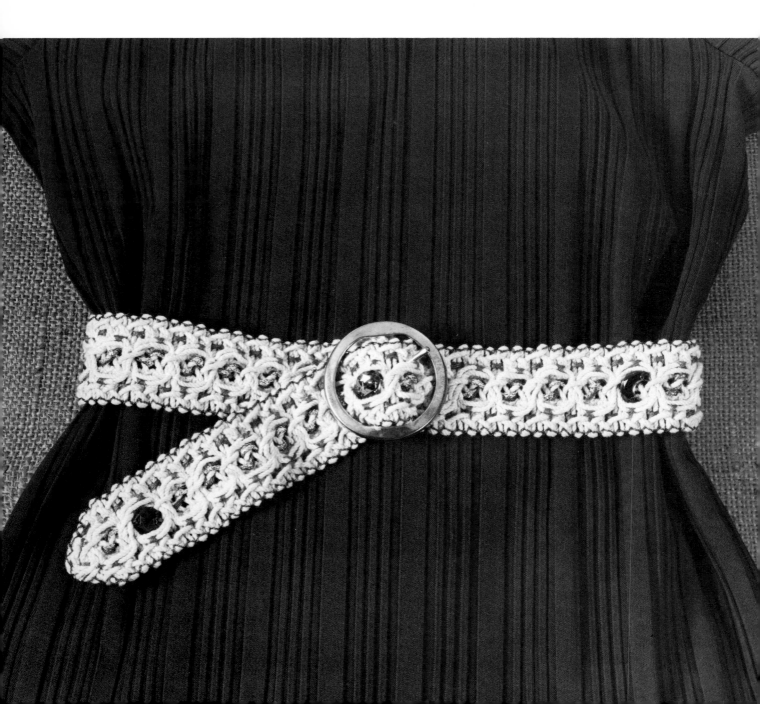

BEDROOM SLIPPERS

Ready-made bedroom slippers come not only in every shape and size, but also in dozens of fabrics. These are nylon and the design was lightly stitched in blue thread.

We worked the flowers in two shades of pink and rose *open chain*. The center is rose *whipped* over the existing blue pattern. Leaves are *stem stitched* in green leaving the existing blue design as a filling.

These were very inexpensive and it seemed silly to spend a great deal of time on them. However, better slippers, using silks and metallic thread, could be turned into Cinderella's favorites.

A BRIGHT BLOUSE

A blouse is always handy to have around. In this day of "separates" it is especially useful. This lovely salmon-and-white Dacron blouse gained a couturier touch, embroidery on a few of the flowers. It is pretty enough for a summer evening skirt and almost too pretty to be hidden under a suit jacket.

The centers called for *squared filling* in dark rosy-red cotton and the centers in turn were outlined with two rows of *buttonhole* —one in maroon and one in the same rosy red using two strands of cotton. Depending on whether you wear this blouse in the day or evening, you might want to work more of the flowers. If it were heavily embroidered and teamed with a silk skirt, it would definitely be very festive, very lovely, and utterly feminine.

A CHECKED DRESS

The little girl's dress of yellow checks has an emblem that was made-to-order for gingham—tic, tac, toe.

The bars were done with three strands of red mercerized cotton in *twisted chain*. The dots are also red, but were worked in *padded satin stitch* to achieve a delightfully raised effect. The "X's" were *cross stitched* in blue to complete the game. More "games" could be scattered all over the dress for added color and amusement.

EVENING SKIRT WITH FLAIR

The ready-made nylon skirt in plate 27 has been upgraded by embroidering selected flowers. The all-over print is fairly busy with its splashes of yellow, pink, white, and sky blue. We kept the stitches to a minimum and yet the added touches made a tremendous difference in the skirt's overall look.

The yellow flowers have whirly centers composed of concentric circles in *twisted chain*, using three strands of blue cotton thread.

The pink flowers have centers filled with *tied-down cross stitches* and are outlined in *buttonhole*, using three strands of red cotton.

The white flowers have centers of green *squared filling*, again using three strands of cotton.

All the flowers decorated are outlined in *buttonhole*, using the same color as their respective centers.

The golden brocade shown on page 35 would make a magnificent evening skirt. The chrysanthemums could be embroidered in a deeper bronze silk—either in an all-over pattern or simply done in a wide panel down the front. Either way the skirt would be regal when teamed with a matching silk blouse. Easy *satin stitches* would give instant results with a minimum of effort. Any of the floral patterns in plates 6, 7, 8, and 9 would be equally effective after receiving your personalizing touch. However, they would present a much more summery appearance.

A Yellow Tablecloth

To show a diversity of materials, let's move on to the yellow synthetic tablecloth shown in plate 21. Here the overall design was very clear and crying out for personalization.

The white flowers were outlined in a dark-green *stem stitch*. Others were simply given orange centers by doing the *buttonhole stitch* in a circle and surrounding it with a *four-legged knot stitch*.

Scattered green stems in *double chain* added weight to the white flowers and leaves. For those who have the time and inclination, all of the white flowers could be worked for a smashing effect.

Cotton thread was used for the embroidering.

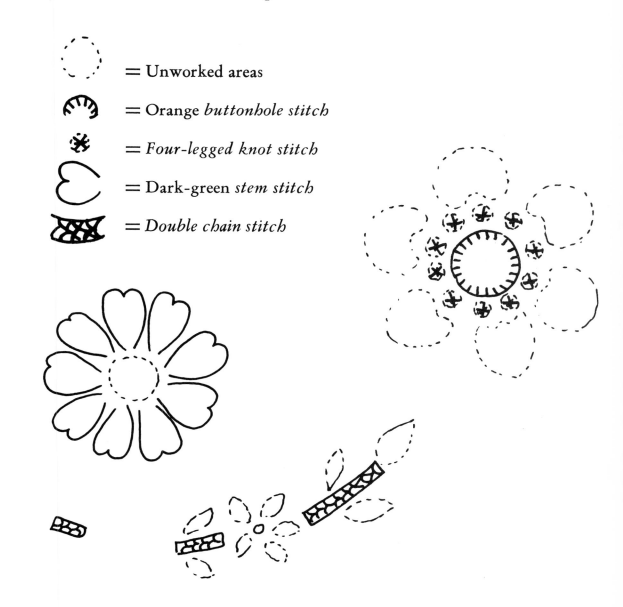

= Unworked areas

= Orange *buttonhole stitch*

= *Four-legged knot stitch*

= Dark-green *stem stitch*

= *Double chain stitch*

A Blue Tablecloth

A second tablecloth (again synthetic), but this time in pale blue, presents a much more countrified air. It is very loosely woven with a netlike feeling and has been dressed up with random daisies in dark blue and white. Here is a perfect example of gaining the maximum effect with the minimum of effort. See color plate 20.

The white outline is in *chain stitch* and the center is composed of a line in a navy-blue *feather stitch*. The same stitchery was used on the napkin.

Imagine how pretty it would be with white milk glass and ironstone china and a bunch of daisies in a center bowl! It looks fresh and summery and has that decorator touch which usually spells expense. However, in this case the tablecloth came from a discount store and the embroidery is solely responsible for its air of costliness.

SHEETS AND PILLOW CASES

Pillow cases may run the gamut from utilitarian to glamorous depending upon your inclination. We have shown two examples of simplified designs for muslin cases. There are beautifully patterned percale cases on the market, but their machine embroidery usually suffices. That is not to say that some couldn't be made more appealing with some handwork, but that is purely a matter of taste and expenditure!

One has dice composed of yellow flowers made by using *satin stitch* and putting *French knots* in the middle of each.

The blue-checked pillow case has the hem outlined in *twisted chain* in two strands of navy-blue cotton. The central navy-blue motif is in *stem stitch* and the outer ones are in a lighter-blue *buttonhole*.

With the hem of the matching sheet embroidered accordingly, you'd have a gay ensemble for any teenager's bedroom.

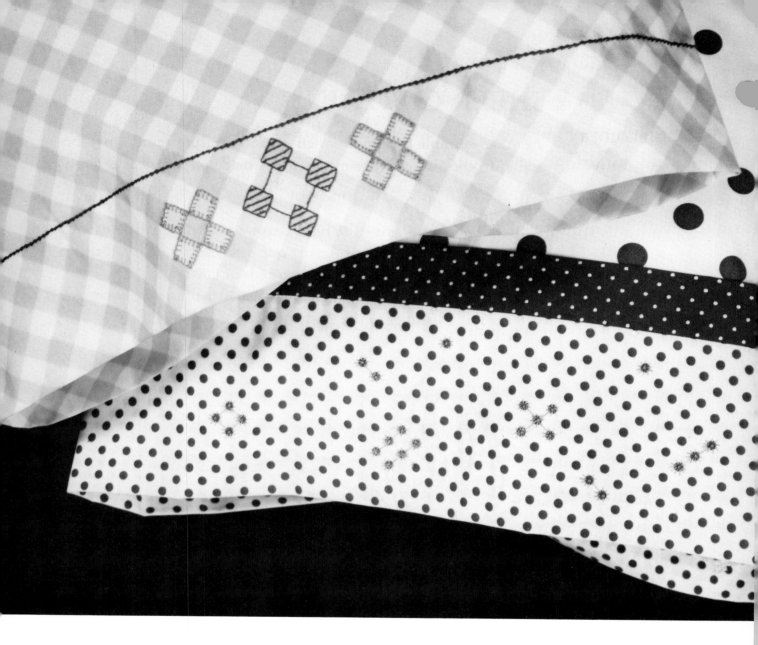

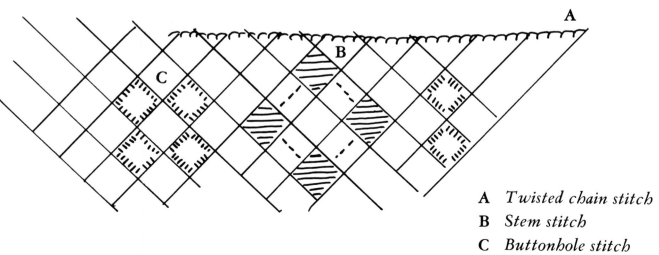

A *Twisted chain stitch*
B *Stem stitch*
C *Buttonhole stitch*

NET CURTAINS

Ready-made and inexpensive curtains seem to proliferate in dry-goods and discount stores. With a bit of leisure time, a bit of imagination, and a small amount of embroidery cotton, you can brighten up your bedroom, bath, or kitchen in no time at all. A tiny word of warning, which is not meant to be a deterrent, merely a whisper of caution. Use *simple stitches* when working on *net*. It is not the most cooperative of fabrics, as it loves to slip and slide, but the finished frothy and airy product is worth the effort.

The second curtains shown are of synthetic net and therefore easy to wash and maintain. The centers of the flowers were done in *stem stitch* using three strands of a peach-pink mercerized cotton. The petals themselves were done in a complementing shade of rusty red in *chain stitch*. Because of the sheerness of the net, only three strands of floss were used at any time—any more would have made the stitches pucker and pull and give messy results.

The small leaves attached to the flowers themselves were done in a light-green *stem stitch*.

The remainder of the leaves and stems were also embroidered in the *chain stitch*.

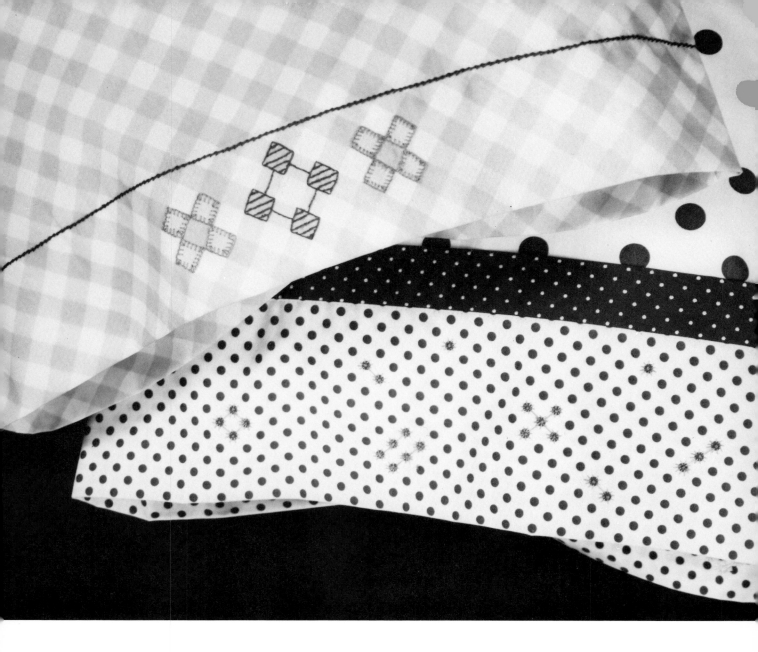
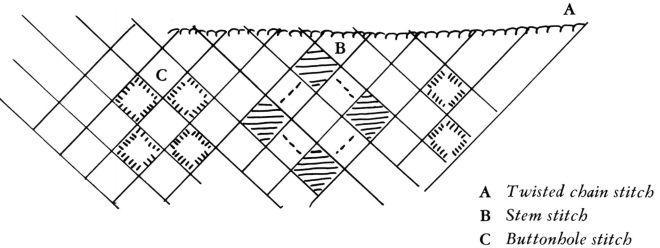

A *Twisted chain stitch*
B *Stem stitch*
C *Buttonhole stitch*

SHEER CURTAINS

Another example of minimum effort and exciting results may be found in these sheer curtains. They are made of practical Dacron and therefore two strands of cotton thread were used in the *chain stitch*.

Blue and white was used to form the two rows of parallel outline. The centers and leaves were already outlined and we *whipped* them in two shades of green (using two strands of cotton).

The stems are, quite properly, done in *stem stitch*, with the stitches lying parallel to the existing lines.

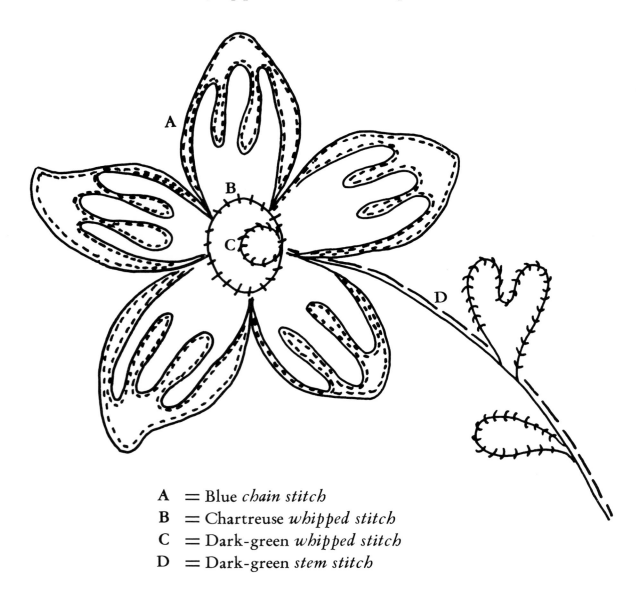

A = Blue *chain stitch*
B = Chartreuse *whipped stitch*
C = Dark-green *whipped stitch*
D = Dark-green *stem stitch*

NET CURTAINS

Ready-made and inexpensive curtains seem to proliferate in dry-goods and discount stores. With a bit of leisure time, a bit of imagination, and a small amount of embroidery cotton, you can brighten up your bedroom, bath, or kitchen in no time at all. A tiny word of warning, which is not meant to be a deterrent, merely a whisper of caution. Use *simple stitches* when working on *net*. It is not the most cooperative of fabrics, as it loves to slip and slide, but the finished frothy and airy product is worth the effort.

The second curtains shown are of synthetic net and therefore easy to wash and maintain. The centers of the flowers were done in *stem stitch* using three strands of a peach-pink mercerized cotton. The petals themselves were done in a complementing shade of rusty red in *chain stitch*. Because of the sheerness of the net, only three strands of floss were used at any time—any more would have made the stitches pucker and pull and give messy results.

The small leaves attached to the flowers themselves were done in a light-green *stem stitch*.

The remainder of the leaves and stems were also embroidered in the *chain stitch*.

LINEN

The fragment of linen with its black and white chinoiserie pictures was chosen to show another field for your endeavors. Here the flowers and trees have been left unadorned but the figures have been highlighted with bright stitchery. They all were done in varying shades of vermilion and crimson single-strand wool using the easy everyday *satin stitch*. Unfortunately the tones of red used have not shown up too well in the photograph but we are presenting it as an idea catcher.

CHINTZ

Bright and busy chintzes are fun for the bedroom but quite often the question arises as to what "goes" with such a multiplicity of artwork. An easy solution to this particular problem is shown on the opposite page. The brilliant green chintz with repeat groupings of white flowers had been used for curtains and a pillow was needed for the matching chaise longue. We embroidered one of the complete floral designs in complementary colors and it added to the overall compatability of the furnishings. Adding a different fabric to the scene would have been fatal as the chintz was too strong to brook any interference! Only a solid color could have survived (or sufficed) and wouldn't have been as interesting as the resulting worked pillow.

The flowers were outlined in pale-pink *satin stitch* using a single strand of wool yarn. Their centers were filled in with salmon *French knots*. The stems are white *chain stitch* with a centering of double-strand *running stitches* in rose. All the leaves were worked in *satin stitch* with a double strand of teal-blue wool.

CONTEMPORARY CHINTZ PRINT

The print in plates 25 and 26 is the epitome of all that's bright and beautiful. It is gay without being gaudy and contemporary to the point of being a classic. Both this sample and the charcoal linen (plate 8) could be used for myriad purposes. Given the right setting, they would both make up into eye-catching pillows. The multicolored chintz could adorn a chair or be a valance over plain white curtains. It could even be utilized for a stunning summer evening skirt.

Relatively heavy yarns were used on this sample to give it added strength and character. If you were to use the same material for a skirt, we would suggest sticking to silk threads and embroidery flosses for a more delicate air.

The large portions of the central blue flowers were filled in with long and short *satin stitches* done at right angles to the long vertical lines. The top blossom was worked with a single strand of pale-blue yarn and the lower was stitched in a darker tone. The very dark areas of these flowers were done in *satin stitch* using a single strand of a very fine forest-green wool. The larger flower has a circle of dark-green *herringbone stitch* and the smaller bloom has a central motif composed of concentric rows of pale-blue *split stitch*. The red-and-yellow daisy at the upper left has its petals outlined in *couching* using a heavy orange silk tied down with a single strand of rust wool. The same rust wool, in a *split stitch*, has been used to form the inner circle. This circle, in turn, has been filled with diagonal *squared filling*, with the basic diagonal lines done in pale green and the tied-down stitches done with one strand each of pale and dark green in the needle. These petals are full of bright-red *French knots*. The other main red flowers were outlined with parallel rows of orange and red with the initial stitches done in peach single-strand wool. The overall stitch is the *Pekingese*. The dark spots are formed of dark-green *satin stitch* and the middle section was done in two shades of green in *squared filling* worked on the diagonal. The open (or unprinted) spaces on the leaves were filled in with two rows of light-green rug yarn, which were tied into place with the *feather stitch* using a single strand of dark-green wool. Some of the leaves were outlined with a single strand of the light-green yarn and tied down with *fly stitches*, again using the forest-green color. Even though the embroidery is different, you gain a continuity of feeling when you use the same color yarns. The larger blue-green leaves have borders of light-green *herringbone*. One or two *tied-down cross stitches* were placed in the middle for interest.

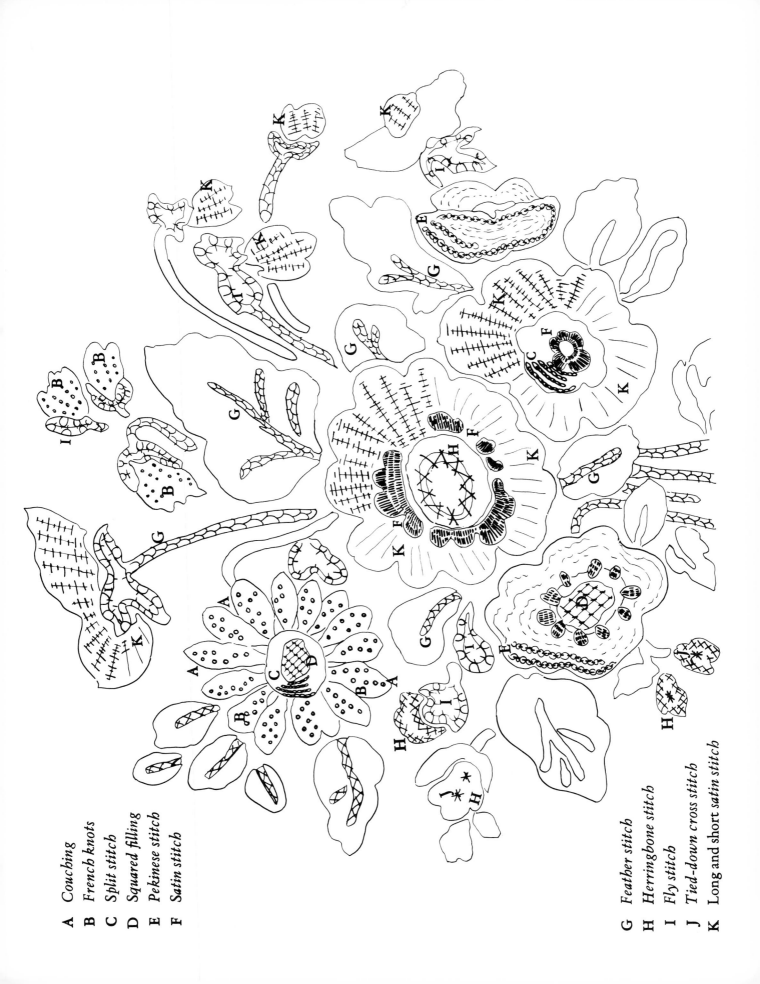

A Couching
B French knots
C Split stitch
D Squared filling
E Pekinese stitch
F Satin stitch

G Feather stitch
H Herringbone stitch
I Fly stitch
J Tied-down cross stitch
K Long and short satin stitch

CHARCOAL LINEN

This strong pink print on charcoal linen is a bit more traditional and would go happily in a den or living room with furniture of almost any period. For the color photo of this print see plate 8.

Here are the directions for the charcoal printed linen. We didn't feel a diagram was necessary, as only two main colors were used. The middle flower and the ones at the top left and bottom right have centers of *Cretan stitch* in pale pink. Their large petals were done in two different types of *squared filling*. (See the stitch diagrams; the difference is readily discernible.) The two remaining flowers were outlined in parallel rows of pink and rose. The inner pink row is *chain stitch* and the outer row is in a rose *open chain stitch*. The pistils are pink *fishbone*. All were done with a single strand of wool yarn.

The centers of the small flowers were worked in *Cretan stitch* in the same two shades of pink and rose.

The veins of the leaves were embroidered differently as follows: The smallest have veins of pea-green *chain stitch*, the triangular leaf was done in *fishbone*, and the big leaf was filled with rows of *chain stitch*. The bottom leaves were done in *chain stitch*. Even though pink and rose are normally regarded as feminine colors, the overall result is strong and masculine. Because of the careful choice of stitches the strength of the pattern has not been diminished one iota.

A PAIR OF SPANISH CHAIRS

Having started the book with two brocaded chairs we will start the last color section with another pair illustrating the same idea, that is, using different stitches on the same fabric to give you a set of interesting chairs which complement each other but escape the boredom of sameness. (See color plates 16 and 17.)

These are antique chairs from Spain and are now beautifully mated to an Old World brocade with up-to-date embroidery. They would be equally beautiful with a satin brocade worked in silk threads—it's all a question of taste and preference. As we show them, they seem a perfect blending of old and new and we hope they will inspire you to whip up a masterpiece of your own right now, this instant!

The colors are clear and strong and show up beautifully against the off-white background of this cotton brocade. A single strand of wool was used for all stitches, which gives a feeling of lightness to the otherwise heavy design. The flowers are in two shades of red with the petals done in *squared filling* with small amounts of *satin stitch for emphasis*. The two flowers at the outer extremities are *satin* and the tips of the petals, which look as if they were turned over, are done in *Cretan*.

The upside-down triangular stem is outlined in chartreuse wool in a *satin stitch* and is filled with gold-toned *couching*.

The large leaves are outlined in green *chain* and are filled with *feather stitching*. They also have darker-green accents in *chain* and *feather*. The checkerboard pattern (which is woven right into the fabric) has been covered over in gold-colored yarn worked in the *satin stitch* in small squares. See plate 17.

First Spanish chair

A *Satin stitch*
B *Satin stitch* in small rectangles
C *Cretan stitch*
D *Squared filling*
E *Couching*
F Outline *satin stitch*
G *Feather stitch*
H *Chain stitch*

As the diagrams on these pages are symmetrical, the colors have been keyed on one side only.

Second Spanish chair

A *Darning stitch* in red
B Gold *satin stitch*
C Gold *buttonhole stitch*
D *Darning stitch* in pink
E *Rumanian stitch*
F *Twisted chain stitch* in
two shades of green
G Red *satin stitch* inserts

The matching chair shown in plate 16 has the flower outlined in dark-red single-strand wool yarn—both in *stem* and *whipped stem stitches*. The body of the flower is filled with *darning* in two shades, one pink and one dark red. The outer two flowers and the turned-over edges are worked in those two shades using the *Rumanian stitch*.

All the leaves are outlined and filled in by using *twisted chain* in both light and dark green. The gold filling in the checkerboard pattern is again done in the *satin stitch*. This is the only exact similarity with the first chair and was demanded by the woven design. The inside triangle is filled with *baby buttonhole* and has been outlined in *satin stitch*.

The completed pair are indeed heirlooms and no ready-made material could complement them to the degree that these hand-embroidered seats have done. For easier execution, you might refer to the diagrams on pages 98 and 99.

Plate 16 Cotton brocade on an antique Spanish chair. See pages 97 and 98.

Plate 17 Seat for the second Spanish chair. See pages 99 and 100.

Plate 18 A folding jewel case worked with wool on cotton brocade. See page 46.

Plate 19 Sunsuit for a little boy and one for a little girl. See pages 74 and 73.

Plate 20 Daisies scattered on a blue tablecloth. See page 86.

Plate 21 Cotton thread decorates a synthetic tablecloth. See page 85.

Plate 22 *Chintz under glass makes an attractive tray. See page 67.*

Plate 23 *Linen embroidered in rust and brown covers the original straps of a luggage rack. See page 104.*

Plate 24 *A portable magazine rack. See page 107.*

Plate 25   Floral chintz "before."
See pages 93 and 94.

Plate 26   The same floral chintz   "after."

Plate 27 *A nylon evening skirt, embroidered in cotton. See page 84.*

Plate 28 *A cotton dress from Taos, New Mexico. See page 51.*

Plate 29 Church embroidery, "The Lamb of God." See page 102.

Plate 30   Altar frontal with golden crosses. See page 101.

The Elegance of Ecclesiastical Embroidery

FOR A COMPLETE CHANGE of subject matter and feeling, let's switch to the ecclesiastical.

One very satisfactory outlet for your embroidery talents would be your church. The cost of church vestments and altar cloths has soared beyond belief, but putting the cost factor aside, how much nicer it would be to make a gift of your time and talent to your parish. The church office usually has a booklet listing shops that carry its related necessities such as linens and fabrics. In an ecclesiastical supply store in New York City we chose two materials in a tightly woven but light silk damask.

GOLDEN CROSSES

The first, shown in plate 30, is in a medium green with a repeat pattern of crosses surrounded by intertwined circles. With the thought of using it for a frontal for the altar, we marked off the center with a pin and worked the circles upward and outward to form one large cross. The circles were done in a dark-green silk *stem stitch*. The inner crosses were *couched* in gold and outlined with dark green *stem* for added delineation. The alternating medallions have the center design worked in *Rumanian stitch*. The inner surrounding motif is *split stitch* and a broken outline is formed by *herringbone stitches*.

This beautiful piece of material could then be *whipped* onto the existing frontal, and gold could be *couched* around the edges for a finishing touch. Or, it could be attached to the drop part of the frontal with small snappers to facilitate the laundering of the altar top.

101

THE LAMB OF GOD

The second piece (in plate 29) is a deep purple with an intricately woven rendition of the "Lamb of God" (*Agnus Dei*). The motif is just about the right size for a covering for the Book of Lessons and when embroidered it would make a glorious gift to your church.

When working on a lightweight fabric be sure that you have even tension on your thread. If it is too loose it will stick up, and if pulled too tightly it will cause the material to pucker.

The I H S (which is the abbreviated spelling of the Greek name for Jesus) was done in *couched* gold Lurex thread—sometimes called *gold work*. This particular stitch done in parallel rows is most effective when a solid look is needed. The lamb was worked with a single row of *couching* giving the desired lighter-looking result.

The grapes, being small, were covered easily with two strands of white silk thread using the *satin stitch*. The grape leaves, to provide variety, were done in two parallel rows of *split stitch*, the outer row being pale mauve and the inner white.

Lines of silver *couching* added interest to the center. The flowers were worked in a pale mauve *satin stitch*. The fleur-de-lis is a symbol of the Virgin Mary. The heavy parts of the flower were done in silver Lurex *couching*. The two leaflike petals were outlined with a single line of silver *couching* and filled in with white silk thread in the *raised stem stitch*. The inset lily was embroidered in pale mauve silk in the *split stitch*. The leaves of the lily were done in *double chain* and *Cretan*.

A frontal of this fabric with five of these groupings in the form of a cross (two vertical and three horizontal) would make an incredibly rich gift that even one of the Three Kings might have en-

vied! It would also enable a group of women to be involved in the project, as I doubt whether one person would want to do the same pattern five times. A piece like this would be a true "labor of love" and a gift to remember for your entire congregation.

A *Couching*
B *Split stitch*
C *Raised stem stitch*
D *Satin stitch*
E *Double chain stitch*
F *Cretan stitch*

Miscellaneous Medley

STURDY LUGGAGE RACK

The closely woven linen with its strong pattern in shades of rust and brown seemed a natural for our mahogany luggage rack (see plate 23).

We cut three strips 1 inch wider than the existing strips and 4 inches longer and took great care to cut them so that the pattern was straight. After embroidering, it was a simple matter to press each side under ½ inch and to tack the ends into place using 2 more inches tucked at each end for added strength; we then whipped the edges over the existing straps. A more difficult way would have been to line the strips and mount them freely—we chose the path of least resistance and felt it made for a stronger rack.

The embroidering involved the *chain* and *herringbone stitches* in three colors (green, brown, and chartreuse), using a single strand of wool yarn. The widest bands are *herringbone*. The triangles and remaining bands are *chain* and the edges were finished in *stem*.

A TOTE BAG

Rummaging around in our odds-and-ends drawer, we came across a fabric with a geometric design. The colors were garish and the design more fitting for an Oriental rug. But the central motif "spoke" to us and it was cut out to be mounted on a plain tote bag. As you can see from the before and after, the results are startling. What was simply a loud fabric has become extremely chic and makes a one-of-a-kind tote bag.

104

The plain fabric (above); embroidered and mounted (below).

To mount, the edges were turned under 6 inches and then the medallion was pinned in place from the center out. Starting at the top center, it was whipped onto the bag—sewing from the inside with matching mercerized cotton. After going from top to half-way on the left side, we switched and went from top center half-way on the right side. This guaranteed a flat and even mounting.

An alternate, and quicker, way of mounting a medallion is by gluing—using an arts-and-crafts glue like Sobo or Elmer's. We would not recommend this method for articles that are to be cleaned frequently—stitching is a more lasting method.

We show both sides of a tote bag. The embroidery is as follows. Starting from the outside using two strands of wool, we made two rows of *split stitch* and formed flowerlike motifs with *double cross stitch*. The small areas of dark brown (at each end) are *satin stitch*. The flowers were outlined in *split stitch* with centers of *satin* and an occasional *tied-down cross stitch*. See opposite page.

The center of the inner flower was done in *satin stitch*. All outlines were worked in *split stitch* with random *French knots* for more diversity.

Believe it or not, the same hunk of fabric that supplied the luggage straps also gave us this elongated medallion for the other side of our tote bag.

This amazing material called forth many ideas. It would have made one woozy to have seen it on a chair, but for our purposes the material was perfect, as it was composed of so many separate design areas. The petaled design would be equally effective on a pillow or a handbag.

The outline looks like two parallel rows, but is *fishbone stitch* done with a single strand of orange yarn.

The yellow bands are *closed herringbone*. The other outlines in rust are both *stem* and *herringbone*. The dark brown is *double knot* using two strands of wool.

For a finishing touch heavy orange braid was *couched* into place for the trim.

PORTABLE MAGAZINE RACK

Children's fabrics are usually busy enough to need no embellishment. However, once in a while you will come across a pattern that cries out with possibilities for myriad different uses. When we first spotted the panda in plate 24, he was on a curtain surrounded by hundreds of his brethren, but we decided that he was strong enough to stand by himself. Thus he became the sole occupant of our magazine rack. As the pattern was heavy, and the cotton tightly woven and firm, we used crewel yarns. Three shades of heavy twisted yarns, ranging in tone from light yellow to light brown, were used on the bamboo.

Couching stitch was used and tied down with *feather stitch*. For emphasis the *feather stitch* was done in a slightly deeper shade of single-strand crewel yarn.

His pink pants called for *raised stem stitch*, also using a single strand of wool. The leaves were outlined in dark-green *stem stitch*. His eyes were brought to greater prominence with the addition of sewn-on buttons, which in turn were outlined with a single *stem stitch* in a dark-gray single-strand wool.

Finale

ALL THE TEDIOUS WORK is done for you when you practice what we demonstrate in this book. There is no designing to be done and no drawing ability is needed. Whatever you do, don't rush. Relax, study your material, and get the feel of it before starting. After you have decided exactly how you're going to use it, choose your colors from the thousands of shades of silks, cottons, and wool yarns that are available in this how-to day and age. That in itself will be fun, as the variety is truly mouth-watering. Once you start embroidering, the fabric will "speak" to you and suggest certain stitches and areas to be worked. You'll find that it is not stereotyped work but truly an artistic outlet and great fun. One piece will lead to another, and as you grow in confidence and see your smashing results, you'll be tempted to do it twenty-four hours a day nonstop.

Above all else, enjoy yourself. We have, and we hope you will, too.

Glossary of Stitches

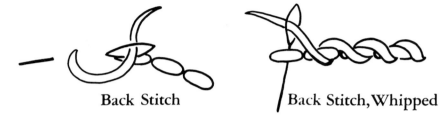

Back Stitch

Back Stitch, Whipped

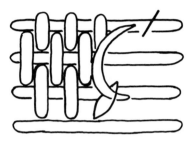
Burden Stitch

Buttonhole Stitch

Chain Stitch

Chain Stitch
Detached

Chain Stitch,
Double

1

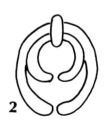
2

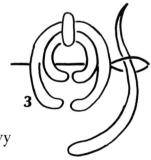
3

Chain Stitch, Heavy

4

Chain Stitch,
Open

Chain Stitch,
Threaded

Chain Stitch,
Twisted

Chain Stitch,
Whipped

Chain Stitch,
Zigzag

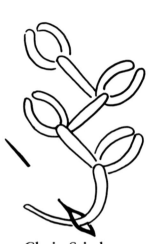

Chain Stitch,
Zigzag-Long-Armed

Coral Stitch

Couching with Cross Stitch

110

Couching with Feather Stitch

**Couching with
Fly Stitch**

Couching with Herringbone Stitch

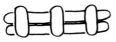

**Couching with
Straight Stitch**

Cross Stitch

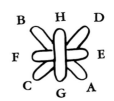

B H D
F E
C G A

Cross Stitch, Double

**Cross Stitch
with Variations**

Cretan Stitch

1

2

Double Knot

**Eye Stitch
or Algerian Eye Stitch**

Feather Stitch

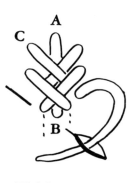

Fishbone Stitch

Fly Stitch

1

2

Four Legged Knot Stitch

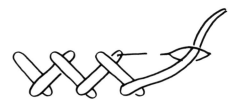

Herringbone Stitch

1

2

Herringbone Stitch, Padded

3

French Knot

Pekinese Stitch

Herringbone Stitch, Tied

112

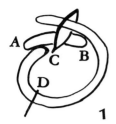

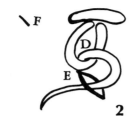

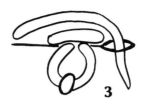

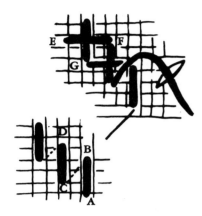

1

2

3

Petal Stitch

Raised Diagonal Band

Rumanian Stitch

Running Stitch

Satin Stitch

Satin Stitch, Padded

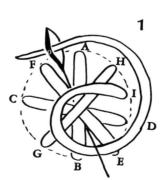

1

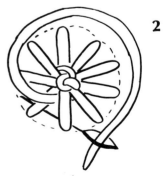

2

Spider Web, Woven

Split Stitch

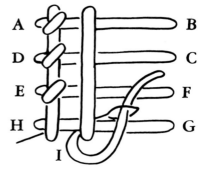

Squared Filling One

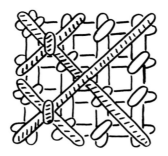

Squared Filling Two

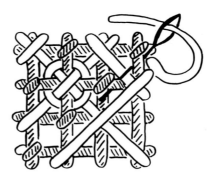

Squared Filling Three

Stem Stitch

Stem Stitch, Raised

Straight Stitch

114

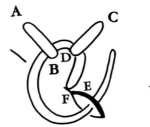

Wheat-Ear Stitch

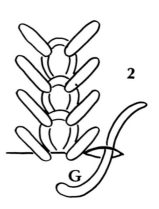

INDEX

Aprons
    with checked border   62
    with daisies   60
    with wings   58
    Zuni   48
Bag, tote   104, 107
Bed linen   86
Bedspreads   39, plates 10, 11
Belt   80
Blanket, baby   71
Blotter, desk   43
Blouse   83
Book cover, moiré   77
    telephone   45, plate 14
Boxes   69
    jewel   42, 78, plate 13
Brocade   5, 10, 34, 36, 37, 46, 69, 97,
        plates 1, 2, 3, 15, 18
Card Case   76
Chairs, antique black   5, plates 1, 3, 15
    Spanish   97-100, plates 16, 17
Chintz   40, 41, 67, 76, 93, plates 6-11, 22,
        25, 26
Cotton   18, 20, 25, 28, 32, 38, 45, 48-51,
        64, 67, plates 4, 5, 14
Curtains   88-90
Damask   44

Dresses
    girl's checked   83
    hand-woven   51, plate 28
    sheath   50
Eyeglass cases   28, 29
Geometric sample   28
Gingham   54-63, 73, 74, 83, plate 19
Golden Crosses   101, plate 30
Hat, straw   79
Headboard   38, 39, plates 10, 11
Ice bucket   64
Jewel box   42, 78
Jewel case, folding   46, plate 18
Lamb of God   102, plate 29
Linen   91, 96, 104, plate 23
Luggage rack   104, plate 23
Magazine rack   107, plate 24
Matchboxes   44, plate 12
Matelassé   22, 31, 32
Moiré   77
Needlecase   25
Pillows
    Design Perfect   19
    Floral cotton, traditional   18, plate 5
    Geometric Jacquard   16
    Pink and orange   20, plate 4
    Satin brocade, flowered   37, plate 2

115

Pincushion   36
Satin   16, 42, 43
Scarf   74
Skirt, evening   84, plate 27
Slippers, bedroom   81
Stitches
    Back   109
    Back, whipped   109
    Burden   109
    Buttonhole   109
    Chain   109
    Chain, detached   109
    Chain, double   109
    Chain, heavy   109
    Chain, open   110
    Chain, threaded   110
    Chain, twisted   110
    Chain, whipped   110
    Chain, zigzag   110
    Chain, zigzag-long-armed   110
    Coral   110
    Couching with cross stitch   110
    Couching with feather stitch   110
    Couching with fly stitch   111
    Couching with herringbone stitch   1
    Couching with straight stitch   111
    Cross   111
    Cross, double   111
    Cross with variations   111
    Cretan   111
    Double knot   111
    Eye   111
    Feather   112
    Fishbone   112
    Fly   112

    Four-legged Knot   112
    French Knot   112
    Herringbone   112
    Herringbone, padded   112
    Herringbone, tied   112
    Pekingese   112
    Petal   113
    Raised diagonal band   113
    Rumanian   113
    Running   113
    Satin   113
    Satin, padded   113
    Spider Web, woven   113
    Split   114
    Squared Filling #1   114
    Squared Filling #2   114
    Squared Filling #3   114
    Stem   114
    Stem, raised   114
    Straight   114
    Wheat-ear   114
Stools   31, 34
Sunsuits, boy's   74, plate 19
    girl's   73, plate 19
Sweater   52
Table mats   70
Tablecloths
    blue   86, plate 20
    yellow   85, plate 21
Telephone-book cover   45, 77
Towel   72
Tray   67, plate 22
Velvet   19, 26, 27, 30
Wall sconce   67
Wastepaper baskets   32, 65